MEET-U

This book is about meetings and providing a new perspective from behavioural economics called nudging to make meetings more productive and enjoyable. Nudging hacks into the fast, automatic, subconscious system in human reasoning to breed success in every get-together. Once you know the foundations of focus, orientation, involvement and commitment, the advantages of nudging are evident. The authors provide an explanation of nudge theory and six principles of how nudging affects our behaviour. Examples from the actions and choices of the Dalai Lama, Ray Dalio and Barack Obama demonstrate how nudging can make a difference. Based on theory, the book also gives 100 very practical nudges to improve meeting productivity that can be used by any meeting leader or participant.

MARTIN J. EPPLER is full Professor of Communication Management in the Institute of Media and Communication Management at the University of St. Gallen, Switzerland. He researches visual practices, meeting management and knowledge management and advises organisations such as the United Nations, the Swiss Re Group, Porsche and the European Central Bank.

SEBASTIAN KERNBACH is Assistant-Professor in creativity at the University of St. Gallen, Switzerland, in the fields of meeting productivity, visual thinking and life design. He is a visiting fellow at Stanford University, USA, coauthored *Creativity in Research* (Cambridge University Press, 2018), and founded the Life Design Lab (www.lifedesignlab.ch).

MEET-UP!

Better Meetings through Nudging

MARTIN J. EPPLER

University of St. Gallen

SEBASTIAN KERNBACH

University of St. Gallen

CAMBRIDGE
UNIVERSITY PRESS

CAMBRIDGE
UNIVERSITY PRESS

University Printing House, Cambridge CB2 8BS, United Kingdom

One Liberty Plaza, 20th Floor, New York, NY 10006, USA

477 Williamstown Road, Port Melbourne, VIC 3207, Australia

314–321, 3rd Floor, Plot 3, Splendor Forum, Jasola District Centre, New Delhi – 110025, India

79 Anson Road, #06–04/06, Singapore 079906

Cambridge University Press is part of the University of Cambridge.

It furthers the University's mission by disseminating knowledge in the pursuit of education, learning, and research at the highest international levels of excellence.

www.cambridge.org
Information on this title: www.cambridge.org/9781108830751
DOI: 10.1017/9781108903059

© Martin J. Eppler and Sebastian Kernbach 2021

First published 2021

A catalogue record for this publication is available from the British Library.

ISBN 978-1-108-83075-1 Hardback
ISBN 978-1-108-82879-6 Paperback

Contents

Figures

Preface

'Let's solve this problem about meetings once and for all'. These were the words of a well-known venture capitalist and former Apple manager from Silicon Valley who had read our research on communication in meetings. He understood the incredible (and often hidden) cost of bad meetings and that meeting productivity was one of the biggest management challenges of our time, as well as a tremendous opportunity. We shared his view that it is not easy to accept that, in the twenty-first century, we are still struggling with the same problems concerning meetings as we were thirty years ago.

After numerous discussions with him and other companies in Atlanta, Boston, Zurich, Geneva, Frankfurt, Lugano and St. Gallen, we concluded that we should try out an entirely new, promising approach to solving the 'meeting problem'. The financier's vision was a strongly technology-driven one, while ours was behavioural. So, after some stimulating exchanges, we parted company with him and started a consortium research project at the University of St. Gallen in Switzerland. Here, we could test and refine a new approach to high-quality meetings with organisations like the European Central Bank and Bank Pictet, as well as public bodies and other non-profit organisations. In this book, we would like to introduce you to this straightforward, tried-and-tested concept.

In addition to several meeting projects and various publications – including an edition on the subject of meetings in the German trade journal *OrganisationsEntwicklung* – we have been able to conduct numerous surveys, experiments and case studies on the quality of meetings over the past three years, some of which you will find in abridged form in this book. We have developed new methods and refined some existing approaches, and some individuals have been particularly supportive along the way. In an amazingly constructive and open atmosphere – Meet-Ups in every sense – we had the privilege of working together with the following people, to whom we offer our sincere and heartfelt thanks: Valérie Saintot and Kristina Friedrich, initiators and coordinators of the

MeetingLAB at the European Central Bank; David Detrey, Francois Conne and Marc Briol of Pictet Asset Services; Professor Michael Hoffman of the Georgia Institute of Technology in Atlanta; and Markus Aeschimann, Michel Binggeli, Dominik Bonderer and Fabienne Bünzli, as well as Stefan Brückner, Martin Bergmann and Claudia Dreiseitel from publishing house Schäffer-Poeschel Verlag.

Since many of us spend a significant part of our working lives in meetings, we should make this critical (life)time productive and positive. Meetings are often the starting points for innovation and change, bringing together expertise and decision-making, detailed knowledge and a broad overview. So let's seize this opportunity to conduct our meetings in a focused, oriented, engaged and responsible manner. It's time to put life into our meetings instead of just enduring them. It's time to expect more from meetings rather than just more meetings! It's time to visualise, orient, involve, challenge and document productively and effectively.

In this book, we will demonstrate how this can be achieved with relatively little extra effort. This is the first publication of its kind to consistently apply the (now Nobel prize-winning) nudging approach from behavioural economics to meetings in organisations. Incidentally, removing the chairs and standing up might be the nudge (more on this term in the book) we need to make meetings more productive. However, there is a wealth of other ingenious impulses for focus, orientation, involvement and responsibility in meetings. Let's explore them together.

Speaking of together, at www.meetup-book.com you can get in touch with us, offer feedback on the book and think more about Meet-Ups. You will also find an interactive overview of all meeting impulses in this book as well as short videos, checklists, useful templates and documents for better meetings. Long live the meeting!

CHAPTER I

Introduction
From Meeting to Meet-Up

Have you ever experienced that feeling? Suddenly the room is full of positive energy and you can build quickly and easily on your colleagues' ideas, while they do the same. You feel valued and are surprised at just how quickly you can make progress, and – as if guided by an unseen force – exchange information, develop ideas, make decisions and initiate measures.

In psychology, such hyper-productive states are called *flow experiences*. As a person or group, you are absorbed in a task and can easily shut out doubts, ulterior motives and distractions. You are focused and committed, but without losing sight of the bigger picture (Csíkszentmihályi, 2010).

Why does this happen so rarely to us? And can we consciously bring about such flow moments in our meetings? Could this happen even if I am not responsible for chairing the meeting and am 'only' attending it?

In this book, we answer such questions (positively!) with a sense of perspective and reality – but also with the courage to seek out unconventional solutions.

In traditional books about meetings, you'll read recommendations such as 'Start and finish sessions on time. Clarify the responsibilities. Avoid deviating from the topic and stick to the agenda'. This is undoubtedly sound advice, but it usually has little effect and falls by the wayside after a short time. *The well-intentioned appeals for better meetings echo in our ears, but the unproductive practices remain.*

So what can you do if unproductive and excessively long meetings are a source of constant irritation and you as a participant, chairperson or external moderator want to break this cycle? The answer is to use *meeting nudges* as smart impulses for changing people's attitudes to meetings. This book is not about mere appeals for change. Instead, we are going to present four tried-and-tested, behavioural levers (which we call cornerstones) to improve meetings effectively and pragmatically – as well as what should happen before and after they take place.

To achieve our ultimate goals, we will be using the well-documented nudging approach from behavioural economics. If we want to encourage our colleagues to take meetings more seriously and achieve more from them, we can do so by making minor changes to the meeting process and its infrastructure. This enables us to gain more *focus*, clear *orientation* in our discussions, more active and constructive *involvement* and a stronger *sense of commitment* before, during and after the meeting. Sooner or later, this will lead to a different and improved meeting culture, away from endless negativity and towards positive solutions – and frequently in a state of shared flow.

Why Meet-Up?

We call this approach to improving meetings **Meet Up!** We chose this term as the title of the book because Meet-Ups in American English refer to (voluntary) focused, relatively informal meetings, which depend heavily on the commitment of participants who want to achieve their common goals as efficiently as possible. In contrast to conventional meetings, Meet-Ups are highly interactive and subtly limit the dominance of individuals through some cleverly designed process and infrastructure changes. Instead of hiding the fact that you are unprepared – after all, managers are brilliant at *incompetence compensation* – or sticking rigidly to an out-of-date meeting agenda, common ground is briefly established at the beginning, and the agenda is clarified and then updated continuously. Distractions or digressions are avoided by involving everyone and responsibilities are visualised for everyone in a way that makes the distribution of tasks transparent and fair. Figure 1 summarises the main differences between such Meet-Ups and traditional meetings.

But the **UP!** in the book title is also a prompt to you, the reader, to get up and allow something which is shared to emerge from your meetings. It is also a promise that productivity and mood will go up when you try out the impulses in this book as a participant or meeting leader. Incidentally, some researchers have shown empirically that there is a direct correlation between meeting quality and employee satisfaction – the better the meetings, the more satisfied the employees. So in countless ways, it makes sense systematically to improve our meetings.

Last but not least, our approach is also called **MEET UP!** because pointing upwards is a pivotal way to get from meeting details back to what is essential – an overview. This is part of a simple conversation navigation method we call *Navicons*, which we are introducing to a wider audience for the first time in this book. With Navicons, you give your discussions a clear direction and signal what kind of dialogue you are having or should be

Aspects	Traditional Meeting	Meet-Up
Participation	Compulsory	Voluntary
Information transfer	Often one-sided	Mostly interactive
Dominant communication methods	PowerPoint, individual verbal contributions	Navicons and sometimes poster-based, associated dialogue
Preparation	Often insufficient and ad-hoc	Motivated by incentives and integrated into the start of the meeting
Agenda	Partly sent in advance or simply not existent	Visualised and prioritised from the start (with Navicons) and continuously tracked
Follow-up	Often unclear and incomplete owing to diffused responsibility	Clear and fast through visualisation and tracking
Duration	Usually one hour (or more)	20–45 minutes
Quality of experience	Poor: monotonous, lengthy, passive	High: varied, compact, interactive, visual

Figure 1 Meetings vs. Meet-Ups

having. This not only helps with communication, but it also saves you from unproductive discussions about tiny details. One of the best impulses for working with Navicons is the humble card or Post-it note. But the Navicon nudge can also be applied through gestures or verbally, as you will see. As a small implementation impulse for these Navicons, we have enclosed a bookmark with this book, which you can start using immediately in discussions (more about this in Chapter 6 on Orientation).

Innovations for Meeting Communication

In addition to Navicons, this book invites you to try out other innovations in meetings. You can use the tips and approaches in a variety of situations – from ad-hoc, one-on-one meetings to monthly departmental or company conferences and from kick-off events to debriefing or lessons-learned sessions. The 100 nudges in this book can be used for training and information events as well as for problem-solving sessions or decision-oriented meetings. For example, you'll learn about the Meet-Up Canvas, a simple session guidance tool, and see how simple PowerPoint hacks from slide presentations can be used to create interactive experiences. You'll see how the Scrumboard easily tracks tasks and obligations and makes them transparent to all present, and you'll experience a new, compact way of minuting meetings – the DOCS Box. In addition to many *analogue* tools, we are also going to introduce you to some *digital* tools for productive meetings, such as Mentimeter.com for quick opinion-forming, surveys and voting.

Specifically, we are going to present nudges or meeting impulses in four areas, which our research and work with organisations has shown to be crucial to successful meetings. Through nudging, you can ensure, or at least improve, the likelihood of each of these four 'cornerstones' at your meetings:

1. **Focus:** You can reduce the number of meetings and radically increase meeting quality (through concentration) by setting helpful targets and focusing on the essentials.
2. **Orientation:** You can use explicit conversation navigation to improve orientation and communication at each meeting.
3. **Involvement:** You can use simple processes (e.g. one-on-one meetings) and (feedback) rules to promote the constructive involvement of everyone at the meeting.
4. **Commitment:** You can use transparency mechanisms to encourage commitment from people at the meeting.

Beyond these core ideas, there are numerous other impulses for each of the four cornerstones, which we present in more detail in this book. Before the small print, however, an overview and what awaits you next.

The Book in Fast-Forward

In Chapter 2, we will present a compact summary of the nudging approach and its scientific and practical background. You will become familiar with different types of nudging and see how these impulses can influence specific behaviour patterns – without forcing anyone's hand or fundamentally altering what motivates them. In Chapter 3, we allow theory to become practice, illustrating from a genuine case study how nudges can change discussions in a positive way. After this real-life application, Chapter 4 then shows – using a simple reference framework (our Meet-

---

↓ **Box 1 – Meeting Misery: The Statistics**

According to an ifo survey conducted in 2014, 88 percent of respondents frequently feel useless during meetings in their company.

A 2011 Harris study came to similar conclusions: 66 percent consider meetings to be inefficient and 40 percent equate meetings with a waste of time. In 2012, Shafer published a survey in which almost half the managers interviewed stated that their productivity would increase radically if they no longer had to attend meetings.

In our own internal company surveys, we have recorded similar values over the past two years. One in three respondents indicated that meetings do not help them with their work but actually interfere with it.

When we asked how much time was wasted in unproductive meetings, the average figure was 45 percent! In other words, respondents reckoned that almost half of their time in meetings is wasted. When asked about the reasons for this inefficiency, the most frequently cited problems were lack of an agenda, dominance by individuals and unhelpful discussions going around in circles. Incidentally, our surveys found that an ordinary employee spends an average of about 8.5 hours per week in meetings. For managers, however, this figure rises rapidly to more than half of the working week; while a study conducted by the management consultancy Bain in 2013 found that senior managers spend more than two full days a week in meetings with three or more employees (Mankins, Brahm & Caimi, 2014).

Up Spiral) – how nudges can be used in meetings. In this chapter, you will also find helpful checklists and a simple self-check of the current 'maturity level' of your meetings.

The main section of this book, however, is from Chapter 5 to Chapter 8. Here, we will introduce you to 100 ways you can improve meetings through simple nudges, whether as a leader or a participant. These chapters are devoted to the four key cornerstones mentioned earlier, and we will differentiate between focus, orientation, involvement and commitment nudges. These chapters will introduce nudges to address questions like those shown in Figure 2.

In Chapter 9, we will summarise our most significant findings, outline necessary framework conditions and venture a look at the future of meetings – Meetings 4.0, so to speak.

We would also like to draw your attention to the Appendix at the back of this book as well as the accompanying *Website*. In the Appendix, you will

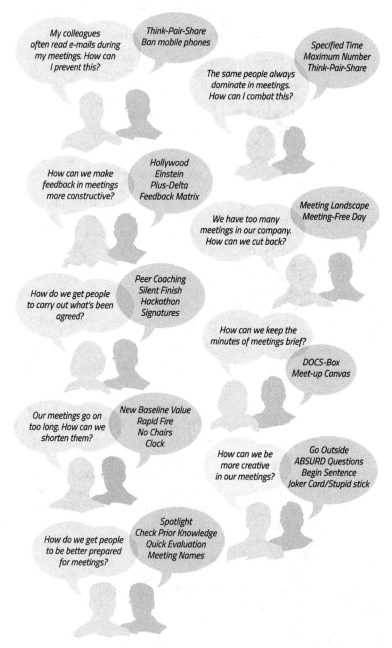

Figure 2 Typical issues at meetings and answers in the form of nudges

find our Meet-Up Manifesto as a mobilisation nudge for posting in corridors or meeting rooms. This will draw attention to the issue of meeting productivity and the desire to improve it. You will also find a simple Meet-Up ABCs in the Appendix, which you could use for internal training. This is a short glossary of the most important terms. In addition, you can use the *signal cards* in the Appendix. You can then use these picture cards as orientation nudges directly in meetings to signal, for example, that a meeting is drifting into details or deviating from its goals. Alternatively, you can download these and other templates from our website at www.meetup-book.com. Give it a go!

Parallel to the main text, you will also find short *information and inspiration boxes* for some lighter reading, where we talk about informative, useful, annoying, curious or simply inspiring ideas for meetings. These boxes show, for example, the secret of successful meetings in Hollywood, typical meeting pitfalls, tips on handling acrimonious meetings and the 'meeting rules' of well-known people such as the Dalai Lama, Jeff Bezos (CEO of Amazon) and Elon Musk of Tesla. Here is an example of just such a box (Figure 2), in this case, proof – if it were needed – that something is very wrong with our business meeting culture and urgent action is required to turn things around.

How to Navigate This Book

To conclude this introduction, a brief note on how to get the best out of this book. You will frequently come across small arrows in the text. These arrows – part of the Navicon method – help to guide you through the text and decide whether you want to read on or skip a paragraph. The four arrows throughout the book indicate the following:

↑ means that this section is an overview paragraph.

↓ means that we are going into greater detail here (e.g. facts, studies, examples).

← means that we are looking back, consolidating experiences and shedding light on the emergence of an idea or a problem.

→ means that this section is about implementation and how to work specifically with the ideas presented.

So we are using the Navicon not only to improve the quality of meetings but also (hopefully) to give you a better, more enjoyable reading experience. We would especially like to recommend the ↑ overview and → implementation sections.

To find the central impulses and solutions in the text more quickly, we have also highlighted all 100 **Nudges** in this book in colour.

Now we would like to invite you to dive with us into the fascinating world of nudging. You will see that the application potential of this approach goes far beyond the way we conduct our business meetings and that you have probably already encountered many nudges in everyday life.

CHAPTER 2

Background
The Nudging Approach for Meetings

Quiz question: What do small plates, pink prisons, flies painted on urinals and organ donation all have in common? And what does any of this have to do with meetings?

Well, all four cases are examples of nudging in action and the same mechanism at work here can also turn your meetings into productive meetings. The idea goes like this:

If we use smaller plates, then the portions appear larger and we feel full faster, meaning we eat less. In a US prison whose cells were painted pink, the number of aggressive attacks fell significantly. Since images of flies began appearing on the urinals in men's toilets at Amsterdam Airport, the floors have been much cleaner (men, it seems, love aiming at something). Similarly, in countries where you are automatically registered as an organ donor and have to opt-out if you do not want to be one, the number of potential donors is much higher than in places where you have to opt-in.

↑ These examples show that counterproductive behaviour can be reduced without coercion through subtle changes in the starting-out (default) position or the infrastructure. So nudges are impulses for action that change people's behaviour in a *predictable way,* but are nonetheless voluntary. The decision to comply is still yours and any economic incentives remain substantially unchanged.

Can we also use this for an area where a better approach is urgently needed, namely meetings? We believe so and, to that end, we have developed and tested nudges – as these clever little interventions are called – for direct application in the meeting context. These nudges are presented in more detail in Chapters 5–8. First, however, we would like to explain the *background* of the nudging approach so that you can recognise, invent and begin to use nudges yourself. To help you develop your own nudges, you will also find some simple *design principles* in this chapter.

← Nudging is an approach to winning people over to (positive) behavioural change by subtly exploiting convenience and misconceptions. Examples include dichotomous (either/or) thinking, mental inertia, an exaggerated fear of loss or a preference for the status quo. The nudge approach is based on a book of the same name by the two (economics and law) professors Richard Thaler (winner of the Nobel Prize for Economics in 2017) and Cass Sunstein, who apply the theory primarily to matters of health care, financial security and consumer decisions (Thaler & Sunstein, 2009). A nudge can also be thought of as a small impulse. Thaler and Sunstein call this (sometimes almost manipulative) approach 'libertarian paternalism', since it does not force anyone to change, but gives subtle impulses for positive change. Many national governments, from Germany and Britain to Canada, have created their own nudges for implementing policy.

↑ The core idea of nudging is based on the conscious design or optimisation of the actual *action and decision situation* in which behavioural change begins. Thaler and Sunstein call this the 'decision architecture', which must be planned and designed in a targeted way so that people choose to change their behaviour. It is essential that nudges do not create any sense of compulsion and do not significantly change the economic incentives of those affected. In other words, it must remain possible to resist or disregard the nudge. So it's not necessarily a nudge when you hear the annoying warning alarm before fastening your car seatbelt.

A Little Nudging Typology

Some nudges are transparent and evident to us (such as in the seatbelt scenario), while others are subtle and go unnoticed; slightly smaller dinner plates may not even be spotted.

In general, nudges are designed either to help us *avoid* unwanted behaviour or to *support* and *encourage* productive behaviour. As already mentioned, they do this through a clearly signalled intervention or through a change that is barely perceptible as a nudge or influence.

→ In the business meeting context, for example, there is the nudge of a mobile phone charge point at the entrance to the meeting room to prevent participants from being distracted by their mobile phones during meetings as they had to leave their mobile phones at the entrance to be charged. This is an example of an avoidance nudge that is barely perceived.

On the other hand, a large countdown timer (as used at Google) or a large clock is an obvious nudge to get participants to be more disciplined about time. An equally obvious nudge to avoid an overlong meeting is to remove the chairs from the room since the meeting will then almost inevitably come to an end after 20–30 minutes. A less obvious nudge to promote a constructive meeting atmosphere is to place stuffed animals, crayons or comics discreetly in the meeting room (e.g. on side tables or by the windows). This demonstrably leads to more constructive behaviour, as we are subconsciously reminded of our childhood and of corresponding rules of conduct such as 'be nice to each other'.

↓ This startling study on the effect of stuffed animals on the cooperative behaviour of people in organisations can also be found in the Harvard Business Review in interview form: **tinyurl.com/y8lyd6qs**

These examples of meeting nudges and nudging types are summarised in Figure 3.

↓ Of course, nudges can also be differentiated in other ways. For example, some nudges explicitly aim to compare our own behaviour with that of *others* while other nudges encourage *self-reflection*. A nudge of the first kind would be a hint such as the following when announcing a meeting on Outlook or similar system: 'Most of your colleagues' meetings take under one hour'.

As a result, you tend to reduce meeting times because you don't want to be seen as more 'wasteful' than your colleagues. You may recognise this approach from the hotel industry. In some hotels, notices state that most guests use their towels for at least two days before having them laundered.

What about the following more self-reflective meeting nudge? The Human Resources (HR) department of an organisation automatically evaluates meeting data from the electronic agenda of each manager and sends out monthly statistics. This allows managers to see how much time they have spent in meetings every month and whether this has increased or decreased (compared

	Avoid	Encourage
Obvious	Remove chairs => Discourages overstaying	Place a large clock or timer on the table or wall => Encourages time discipline
Not obvious	Charging station for mobile phones place at the entrance => Avoiding distractions	Seemingly random placement of objects that remind us of our childhood =>Encourages appreciative communication

Figure 3 A simple typology of nudges for the meeting-room situation

to the previous month). As with calorie counters or step measurements, this leads to a desire to improve – which in our case means a reduction in meeting hours.

↑ These examples give you a taste of the approaches we have used in this book to improve the quality of meetings. The ingenious thing about the nudging approach, however, is that we don't have to limit ourselves to a finite set of interventions. The nudging approach also offers you a kind of *construction kit* with which you can design your own impulses that take account of your specific situation and context. In the following section, we will give you some simple tips for creating nudges for meetings (and perhaps even beyond). But why are nudges needed in the business meeting context at all? Because without them, we often find ourselves victims to (at least) one well-known meeting pitfall – the 'common knowledge effect'. You must have come across this annoying problem already since it is one of the root causes of unproductive meetings (see Box 2).

Design Principles for Nudges

How do you create even simple impulses that can result in more productive meetings for you and your colleagues? The literature on nudging helps us answer this question because it has identified some ingenious mechanisms to promote or discourage certain types of behaviour relatively easily and effectively. We have formulated these insights from nudging research into six simple principles that can help you turn any meeting into a Meet-Up.

↑ These six design aids are the *default value principle, the pre-structuring principle, the feedback principle, the signalling principle, the fun factor principle* and *the mistake avoidance principle*. Each of these six principles suggests clues and ideas to create effective impulses for better meetings. Let's take a closer look at each of these principles in terms of their underlying insights, applications to date and implementation in the meeting context. You will then find more detailed information and implementation tips for each of the nudges mentioned in Chapters 5–8 of this book.

Last but not least, we also offer a reflection question for each principle as a kind of nudge to help you apply these six principles in daily practice. These questions also help you to think further about the principle and how to apply it in different situations.

↓ **Box 2 – Meeting Pitfall: The Hidden Profile Problem**

It sounds paradoxical, but it's true. We waste a lot of time in meetings because we tell each other what everyone already knows. Groups tend to discuss information that is known to the majority of participants before the meeting even begins, while facts known to just a few participants are seldom shared, so they do not contribute towards solution-finding. This hidden knowledge or 'hidden profile' is not revealed and the group does not benefit from the diversity of its members because they do not share their particular expertise.

Social psychologists Garold Stasser and William Titus have demonstrated through numerous experiments that group members do not exchange individual (relevant) information (Stasser & Titus, 2003). This effect becomes more pronounced when exclusive information deviates from the majority opinion. But how can this be explained? In short, we generally prefer facts that support our original viewpoint; information which is known to all participants seems to be more valid and confirms what everyone already knows. Exclusive information from individuals, on the other hand, adds additional and sometimes contradictory aspects and attracts criticism. At the same time, discussion partners continuously compare their positions and information and estimate how these are viewed by their colleagues. If they see that their opinion is shared by others, they feel confident enough to make their conclusions more strongly felt. One way to solve the hidden profile problem is to ask participants to share their views with the chairperson in a short email before the meeting. The chairperson can then activate the participants as he or she knows about their potential contribution. What helps in addition to this nudge, of course, is to stay true to yourself and be prepared to share controversial or disagreeable information at meetings.

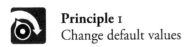

Principle 1
Change default values

Insight

People are strongly influenced by their default values (i.e. predefined options) because it takes a lot of effort to change them. Default values are like mental anchors from which it is very hard to detach ourselves.

Practical Examples

If a company's standard printer settings are changed to make printing double-sided, paper costs are massively reduced. If 30 per cent 'green' electricity is given as a default value, many more households will choose this energy source than if no default value is proposed.

Implementation
Set the default value for the duration of meetings (in Outlook or on paper) to 45 minutes (instead of one hour). Alternatively, set the default value for jobs per person to two (in the agenda/minutes or on a flipchart during a meeting), so that everyone can expect to receive two tasks and cannot avoid some responsibility. You could also make the agenda (including goals and necessary information) a mandatory attachment when issuing invitations to meetings.

Pause for Thought
What specific opportunities do I have to suggest new default values that would help save time, money or effort?

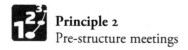 **Principle 2**
Pre-structure meetings

Insight
People tend to follow pre-structured (decision-making or action) paths. It is more convenient to stick to a simple procedure than invent a new one.

Practical Examples
In some streets, steps are painted on the pavement so that you follow them directly to the litter bin. In London, many pedestrian crossings have signs telling you to 'Look Right'.

→ Implementation
Visualise the meeting agenda on a flipchart (goals and steps to get there) and ask your colleagues if they agree. Alternatively, if you want to make conscious decisions in a meeting, it is advisable to prepare the possible alternatives as decision-making templates on a PowerPoint slide. You could also give your colleagues a simple flowchart that shows when it makes sense to convene a meeting.

Pause for Thought
What recurring processes in the meetings I lead or attend could be improved with pre-structured procedures?

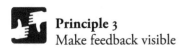 **Principle 3**
Make feedback visible

Insight
Feedback on the achievement of goals strengthens personal commitment as well as self-reflection. Visible feedback – especially when visible to every-one – creates a subtle push for improvement.

Practical Example
Busy residential areas use digital boards on which drivers can see their actual speed. If their speed is within the legal limit, the digits flash green or a smiley face appears.

→ Implementation
At the very beginning of key meetings, place an evaluation sheet for the session on the table so participants can give feedback about whether they felt the meeting was necessary and efficient, and whether they made a useful contribution. Alternatively, for each agenda item, briefly check whether you have kept to the time allocated for it.

Pause for Thought
Which indicators always help us as a team to improve our meetings (e.g. number of problems solved or decisions made)?

 Principle 4
Sharpen perceptions through signalling

Insight
We unconsciously filter out a lot of (relevant) information and do not necessarily perceive essential things, so we must emphasise important information.

Practical Example
In Switzerland, to draw the attention of motorists to pedestrian crosswalks, these are sometimes fitted with light reflectors.

→ Implementation
Place an egg timer on the table or a large clock on a clearly visible wall to indicate the time already used. Give your colleagues the cards in the Appendix of this book so they can signal when a subject is well-known or unproductive.

Pause for Thought
What key information could I make more obvious using a poster in our meetings?

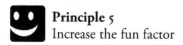 **Principle 5**
Increase the fun factor

Insight
We all prefer the activities we enjoy. We are more committed and better focused.

Practical Example
To encourage commuters to walk instead of using the escalator, the Brussels Metro has turned some of its steps into piano keys (Figure 4).

→ Implementation
Instead of everyone taking turns to introduce themselves at the beginning of a kick-off meeting, participants take an object out of a suitcase and use it – and a little imagination – to introduce themselves to the group (e.g. what does this toy have in common with me?) Alternatively, instead of presenting the status of their own projects as a series of slides, they could interview each other briefly or do speed rounds where everyone speaks about his or her project for one minute only. You could also hold the meeting outdoors (weather permitting) – nature is a great nudge for creative ideas.

Figure 4 Increasing the fun factor of climbing stairs (Montgomery metro station in Brussels) (Source: The Oval Office)

Pause for Thought
Are there any activities in our meetings that I could organise in a more fun way? How might my colleagues react?

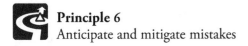 **Principle 6**
Anticipate and mitigate mistakes

Insight
Much that is down to human error can be anticipated and avoided – or at least mitigated.

Practical Example
People can easily forget to retrieve their bank card when withdrawing money from an ATM. Consequently, machines are designed so you must first remove the card before any money is dispensed.

→ **Implementation**
Anticipate that people will forget tasks or be unprepared for a meeting by sending short email reminders a day in advance. On the attached agenda, indicate that each participant will first be asked for feedback on their assigned tasks.

Pause for Thought
What typical oversights before, during or after meetings can I help prevent?

Of course, we are aware that in reality, many nudges cannot be assigned neatly to just one principle. Indeed, many impulses draw on several principles at the same time. Nevertheless, the six principles outlined here help to create targeted impulses for improvement and inventing new nudges.

→ For example, start with just one principle to develop a nudge and then try to use other principles to improve it. Then test your nudges in small team meetings before moving on to larger gatherings. In the following chapter, you will see how this might look in a case study of nudging in business meetings. Here, we have incorporated some of our experiences from various organisations into a single story.

CHAPTER 3

Case Study
Meet-Ups in Practice

'I. Love. This. Meeting!' announced Rea's boss to the assembled group. Rea looked at him in disbelief. Astonished, her colleagues looked at Rea. How had she managed to convert the notorious pessimist Ian Hampton into a dedicated Meet-Up practitioner in a matter of minutes? What had happened?

Just a week ago, Rea Yunen was standing in her new boss's office being told that he'd had enough of spending more than ten hours each week in unproductive meetings. Without further ado, he appointed her chairperson (he even used the term 'meeting magician') of the team to 'sort out this mess'. She was astonished. She had not envisaged anything like this when she applied for the post. How could she do it? Was she capable of changing a fossilised meeting culture? What difference could she – a small cog in a big wheel – make?

That evening, even her yoga teacher noticed how tense Rea was and how her mind seemed to be somewhere else. The headstand, which usually went so well, just didn't want to work today. 'What's the matter?' the teacher asked after the class, to which Rea merely replied, 'Oh, just stress at work'. The next day Rea sat down, as usual, in various meetings and tried to observe the behaviour of her colleagues more closely. Somehow, she had to figure out a way to improve these meetings and quickly. Her boss was absolutely right; there was a lot of talking, but nothing was ever decided. Certain people dominated the discussion, an agenda was either not available or already abandoned after two minutes because some issue was dissected down the smallest detail. Frustration was the order of the day. It couldn't go on like this, but how could she change it? Rea had never felt this confused before and it worried her.

Rea worked in the transaction team of a large bank and was responsible for working practices and service quality within the framework of the 'Work 4.0' initiative. As a digital native, she searched online for new digital ways to improve in-house meetings. She found many websites saying things like 'begin meetings on time', but there was no specific advice on how to do this.

Frustrated and with expectations of her boss still ringing in her ears, she dragged herself into the team's breakroom that afternoon. While she sipped on her latte macchiato, she made a little observation that would change everything. At the adjacent coffee bar, she saw three colleagues animatedly discussing a print-out. It really seemed to be a productive exchange and this gave Rea an idea. The following morning, she cleared the chairs from the meeting room in the hope that **Stand Up** would have the same effect she had noticed the night before. People were initially sceptical and one of her colleagues even said, 'I have to stand on the bus every morning and now here too?' Rea blushed. Had her idea been too radical? But she stuck to her guns and what followed was amazing. The discussion was indeed more intense than in the past and everyone present seemed to be more focused when it came to making decisions. At the end of the meeting, everyone was surprised that instead of the usual hour or more, this meeting had only taken 40 minutes. The usual moaning and groaning failed to materialise either. Instead, a colleague remarked, 'and I still have time for a second coffee'. Rea took a deep breath, went back to her desk and sank onto her chair visibly relieved. 'That went quite well', she thought when a colleague ran by with her thumbs up and said, 'Standing up only from now on, please!' Rea summed it up: 'Yes, this is Work 4.0, but it doesn't always have to be about technology. Obviously, you can trigger real changes in small non-digital ways as well.' Now she was on fire to try out more new ideas.

At the next project meeting in the afternoon, she wrote the agenda on a clearly visible flipchart so everyone knew where they were. Rea had copied this technique from Sheryl Sandberg at Facebook, who did it on her notepad although this was not visible. But then a colleague said he would never write on flipcharts with his chicken scratch, which dampened Rea's spirits. But she did not give up and simply replied, 'then get a colleague on your team to write for you'. Everyone agreed that a **Visible Agenda** gave much-needed structure to the meeting. When they reached the agenda item 'Success factors for future projects', Rea delivered a real shocker. 'How about ensuring all projects *fail?*' There was dead silence in the room. Everyone looked at each other aghast as Rea took a deep breath. 'And then we look at how we can generate the success factors from these negative aspects.' Rea had put all her eggs in one basket, but she wanted to go through with it. 'Now, each person should think up at least five failure factors [Figure 5] on their own and then get into **Pairs** to

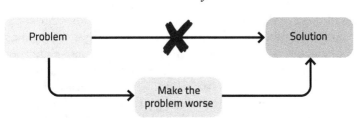

Figure 5 Solving problems by making them worse

exchange ideas. Then they have to find a minimum of one positive factor for every ten negatives and afterwards present their best three positive factors to the rest of the meeting.'

With an imperceptible nod, the boss indicated that Rea had his support. She had previously told him about the success of the **Think-Pair-Share** method for pre-structuring the generating of ideas. So the eight project leaders began to write down their thoughts and the effect was amazing. Working in pairs, the discussion was lively and new ideas came thick and fast. The plenum exchange was also very productive because of the **Specification** of three ideas per team, meaning everyone had their say. Despite this, the project leaders did not want to appear too enthusiastic because they hadn't come up with the idea of turning unproductive plenary discussions into two-person dialogues. One project manager even said that this was 'very close to manipulation – but it was for a good cause'. Another couldn't resist adding: 'Being destructive is great fun!' A little bit of praise for Rea, but she was happy and at the same time, very excited.

What she had achieved in that team meeting had happened despite all the reservations and initial doubts of her colleagues. Through small changes, she could help everyone to be more productive in meetings by direct – and sometimes subtle – intervention.

But it was only now that the greatest challenge, the one Rea had been dreading, arrived – a general meeting of the Board of Directors – and this was important for her boss. Passing Rea's office late in the evening, he reminded her: 'We need two or three good ideas for the meeting tomorrow afternoon. Come to my office for a preliminary meeting at 9 a.m.' It was now 7 p.m. and Rea was tired and hungry. How could she come up with more exciting ideas for this demanding group by tomorrow morning?

Just then, a reminder popped up on her mobile phone about a meeting of the executive committee of her professional association in one hour. Oh, no! Rea had forgotten entirely about this appointment. Rea had had enough of these endless sessions which often went on long into the night. What could she do? She was in the chair that night, so sending her apologies was out of the question. On the way to her late-night meeting, she bought herself a sandwich, which she ate in the parking lot, lost in thought. Then she had an inspired idea – why not leave these endless discussions about details in a metaphorical parking lot and return to them later? So tonight the group would discuss the business of the evening in a focused way and not constantly digress. Arriving at the meeting, Rea drew a large P for parking on a flipchart and prepared blank Post-it notes to record irrelevant issues. During the meeting, she wrote down all the new, non-agenda items that the participants felt they 'must, should, or could' discuss. This actually made the meeting more productive and the discussion more focused. Rea had considered having the meeting without chairs, but that would have been too much of a good thing after a long working day. Despite sitting down, everyone was on their way home by 10 p.m., which had not happened in recent years. Rea looked back with satisfaction on an eventful day, but the joy was only short-lived, as she still had her boss and tomorrow's board meeting in the back of her mind.

As she lay in bed, Rea tried to distract herself and recalled her dream of one day opening a gallery, but at the same time and despite her best efforts, the image of the management board meeting kept springing up. She woke early the following morning after a restless night. 'Why not turn a meeting room into a gallery?' she thought half asleep as she took a shower. On her way to work, she read in a management magazine about the ability of Navicons to structure conversations on complex topics and to help participants engage in real dialogue.

Rea combined these thoughts and a short time later, she presented both ideas to her boss. First, the **Gallery Walk**, where the key slides were exhibited in poster format to give the Board of Directors the chance to move from one to another at their own pace while discussing them. At the same time, each poster had space for comments and additions that could be added by pen. **Navicons** would be available in the form of Post-it notes with arrows. Thanks to the Navicons, each board member would have the opportunity to indicate whether there was a need for more context information or the big picture (up arrow), more details and facts (down arrow), a review of past situations (left arrow) or questions about the impact and future implementation (right arrow). Rea's boss was enthusiastic about the Navicons, but extremely sceptical about the Gallery Walk. 'You're introducing this', he said, 'and take care with the posters. If this fails, then we'll need the slides as a backup, and . . . ' – he peered at her over the top of his glasses – 'you're going to have a problem'. Rea swallowed hard and wondered if perhaps she'd gone too far this time. What had she got herself into? Were her ideas too radical? But it was all or nothing now, so Rea kept herself busy by printing out the posters and organising pens and Post-it notes.

That afternoon, the board meeting started with the usual agenda until Rea's boss announced a change of format and gave Rea the floor. Her heart was racing as she asked the directors to stand up and walk to the first poster. She explained the idea of the Gallery Walk and the function of the Navicons. 'I'm not at the Tate Gallery – what's the point of this?' someone whispered. But by then a discussion about the first enlarged slide had begun and Rea's boss used the pens to note down the ensuing comments and questions. The debate became animated and time flew by so quickly that Rea had to remind her boss and the group to move on to the next poster. Now people began picking up pens – reassured that drawing skills were not needed and that they had everyone's attention when they were talking and writing at the same time. After some initial hesitation, the Navicons began to be used, especially the upward arrow when some of the group became embroiled in discussions about tiny details.

Rea's boss was clearly impressed, but did not let on. 'It was okay', was all she got out of him at the end of the meeting. Baffled, Rea accepted the guarded compliment but was also annoyed. Was she alone in thinking that the meeting had been much more positive than she'd dared to hope?

Over the weekend, she tried to distract herself but didn't really succeed. What a strange adventure, she thought. This week she had experienced lots of lows but also a few highs. She needed to motivate herself to find new ways to improve meetings and then she would talk to the boss again.

At the Monday morning meeting, she again took away the chairs and gave the group creative questions about how to reach Generation Y through marketing. For example, one group was asked to consider the question: 'What would we do if money didn't play a role?' and another: 'What solution would we *never* suggest?' Inspired by these **Unusual Questions**, there were some lively group discussions and even fun to be had. When the first group had finished presenting their ideas, something unexpected happened.

Suddenly Rea's boss stood up and announced: 'I. Love. This. Meeting'. Rea looked at him in disbelief. Astonished, her colleagues looked at Rea. He described her as a 'genius' who had brilliantly made every meeting unique. Only now did he thank her for the great ideas she had brought to the board meeting, and Rea couldn't help but breathe a huge sigh of relief.

Figure 6 Rea Yunen reflects on her ideas for improvement

Now, the spell had been broken. Colleagues came to Rea with new ideas, such as the meeting app for interactive queries and instant visual surveys – **Mentimeter** – which was soon to be tried out in the sales meeting. Rea began to develop a meeting toolbox. A few days later, her boss said: 'And next week we'll have a **Meeting Tabula Rasa**. We can question the need for all these meetings, meeting attendance should be voluntary, and we'll make one day each week meeting-free.'

Rea thought over the past few weeks. Thanks to her *courage*, she had managed to give a new direction to the meeting culture of her team. She had pushed the boundaries in some cases with significant changes, such as the Gallery Walk in the management board meeting, but she had also been able to achieve a lot with small impulses, such as the Visible Agenda, the Parking Space for ideas and No Chairs. Sometimes she had tried something out on her own initiative and sometimes she had run ideas past her managers first. She realised that you don't have to be the boss or chair-person to try out new things. Anyway, she now knew that the best way to persuade sceptical colleagues was by giving them the chance to experience these innovations for themselves. Rea achieved this by giving direct *instructions*, such as having conversations in pairs, which were initiated through new procedures and rules, but also by more subtle encouragement (such as meetings without chairs), which she achieved by altering the *infrastructure*.

Last but not least, Rea realised that even with tiny changes, a certain amount of courage is needed to introduce changes to procedure or infra-structure, to change the mindset of her colleagues towards meetings or, as her boss put it, 'to bring meetings kicking and screaming into the twenty-first century'. And with that, Rea's headstand in yoga worked again (Figure 6).

Meet-Up Model
Four Cornerstones for Better Meetings

← Perhaps you found the story in Chapter 3 a little over-dramatic, and you prefer things to be clear, concise and ordered. If so, then Chapter 4 is for you.

↑ In this chapter, we will give you a systematic overview of the Meet-Up approach and its four types of impulse across the different phases of a meeting. We will also show you how these four cornerstones interact and what you can expect in Chapters 5–8. Furthermore, you can use the simple frame of reference in this chapter as a diagnosis and evaluation tool to gauge the current state of your business meetings. Above all, however, the spiral in this chapter is a simple way to visualise the success factors of meetings, to use them as a checklist or to create your own nudges.

Of course, you are free to cherry-pick and simply select your favourite nudges from Chapters 5–8 and implement them. Nevertheless, we believe it makes sense to treat all these nudges systematically before using them individually or in combination.

We hope that this approach will *democratise the conduct of meetings* and *empower* everyone taking part. The expression 'shared leadership' is used in management literature, and our approach is, therefore, deliberately directed not only at those leading meetings but at anyone concerned about the effectiveness of meetings. Some of the nudges in this book also function as passive moderators, that is, they take on a coordinating role and help participants to organise themselves and move forward.

As mentioned in Chapter 1, in our research and work in the field, we identified four aspects critical to productive, fruitful and enjoyable meetings. These four factors – we call them Meet-Up cornerstones – not only help a group to move forward quickly in terms of *content*; they are also essential in doing justice to the *social aspects* of business meetings.

A meeting is not only for coordination or information but it is also an opportunity to cultivate or deepen relationships with colleagues. Any approach to improving the overall quality of meetings must take this into account.

To ensure the success of a meeting in terms of both content and interpersonal relations, we suggest four cornerstones – impulses for more *focus* on and during meetings, assistance for shared *orientation*, ideas for more (constructive) *involvement* and *commitment* (in the sense of accepting responsibility).

In other words, if you succeed in strengthening focus, orientation, involvement and commitment in your meetings, then a high level of productivity is an almost guaranteed by-product.

To sum up in four sentences:

Focus
Meetings only work with (ongoing) concentration on the essentials, even if that sometimes means cutting back; otherwise, you will get bogged down.

Orientation
Meeting content needs clear navigation to avoid wasting time and creating confusion.

Involvement
Constructive involvement must be actively promoted and shaped; otherwise, the same people will always dominate.

Commitment
For all visible, individual responsibilities and shared undertakings, ensure that what has been agreed upon is implemented.

Since these four cornerstones for increased productivity in meetings are not straightforward demands, we need to use simple nudges to help us achieve the desired outcome. That's what this book is about. From our experience, a problem-and-phase-oriented approach is right, and we will introduce this to you in the following sections.

Starting Point: Problems and Phases in Meetings

← How did we arrive at these four cornerstones, you may ask yourself. The short answer is that we analysed the dominant meeting problems we identified in our research and that of our academic colleagues (see, for example, Allen et al., 2015). In interviews, observations and experiments, the same problems in meetings arise time and again:

1. **A missing focus**: Meetings are not goal-oriented. Discussions take place in a circle and participants wander off topic. People are not concentrating and can be distracted. Part of this problem is also that meetings are unfocused and take place far too often – even if there are other options (e.g. an e-mail containing all the necessary information).
2. **Confusion about the current topic and course of the discussion**: It is not clear what type of conversation is taking place. This leads to misunderstandings and people talking over each other.
3. **Lack of or non-productive involvement**: Individuals dominate while shared expertise and creativity are not activated or used. Instead of sharing or developing new knowledge, all the known facts are simply repeated (see also Box 2).
4. **No clear responsibilities**: At the end of the meeting, it is unclear what has been decided or who is responsible for any further action.

→ To solve these problems, we should not only focus on the meeting itself but also consider what happens – or should happen – *before* and *after* a meeting. During the meeting, we can then distinguish between the (hopefully punctual and motivating) beginning, the interactive middle and the concluding items (Figure 7).

Focus is particularly important when calling a meeting. Do you really need a meeting? Who ought to be present? What is the central topic being discussed? But even during the meeting, it is crucial to remain focused and on-target.

Orientation as an antidote to confusing conversations is vital at the beginning as well as during a meeting. What should be discussed first and in what way?

Where must you go into detail and where should you reflect? What has already been sufficiently discussed and what remains to be decided? It is precisely these questions we will be answering using the Navicon approach and other orientation nudges.

Involvement is crucial, especially in the middle phase of a meeting, to introduce as many perspectives, experiences and ideas on a given topic as possible. Do you want to encourage involvement directly through procedures and rules? Or do you want to use infrastructure and artefacts to entice the participants in a more subtle way? The nudges in this chapter will help you come to a decision.

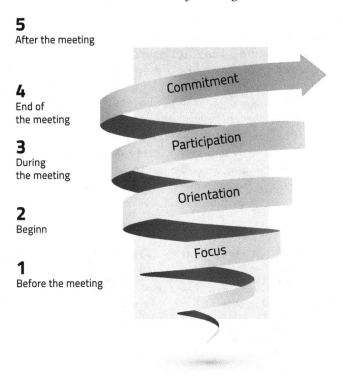

5
After the meeting

4
End of
the meeting

3
During
the meeting

2
Beginn

1
Before the meeting

Figure 7 The Meet-Up spiral through the meeting phases

Finally, **Commitment** is the key to a successful conclusion and the effective implementation of what has been decided at a meeting. Do you want to use direct requests and reason to persuade people to accept tasks? Or do you want to motivate them with the help of transparency and fairness? With these nudges, you can create a positive culture of commitment in your meetings.

A Phase Model of Meetings

The most important phases of a meeting are the before, the start, the middle, the end and the after. Each of these phases has specific challenges and success factors that you can influence through nudging (Figure 8).

A nudging tactic can be particularly effective for a given phase, such as changing default values before the meeting to encourage shorter meeting times (e.g. suddenly 30 minutes is the new standard for meetings). The fun factor is especially useful in the middle of a meeting to maintain the attention and motivation of all participants.

A playful moment in the middle of a meeting can also help to involve participants. At the end of a meeting, it is essential to signal what tasks are still waiting to be assigned and who has not yet contributed.

Figure 9 shows the challenges, success factors and useful nudging approaches for each meeting phase.

Now we can assign any serious meeting problems to a phase and tackle them using a corresponding Meet-Up feature or nudging approach. This is summarised in Figure 9, together with the symbols for the nudging principles.

Phase	Typical meeting problems per phase	Success factors or nudging goals	Main factor and nudging tactics
Before the meeting	Too many meeting invitations, lack of preparation, no preliminary information, too many participants, unclear aims	Focus on necessary meetings and key goals, recognise commitment and make motivated preparations	Better focus using new baseline values
Beginning of the meeting	Participants arriving late, unclear agenda or agenda not aimed at those present	Orientation and understanding/consent to the goals and steps to achieve them	Focus and orientation through pre-structuring
During the meeting	One-sided participation, confusing discussion process, drifting into irrelevant details	Orientation of the discussion process and participation by all	Orientation and participation using the fun factor and signalisation
End of the meeting	Running out of time, items not discussed, unclear what happens next	Time reserve for planning, clarity regarding responsibility and next steps	Commitment through feedback and signalling
After the meeting	Agreements forgotten, lack of personal responsibility	Respecting the actions and responsibilities agreed	Commitment through error avoidance

Figure 8　Meeting phases including their challenges and solution approaches

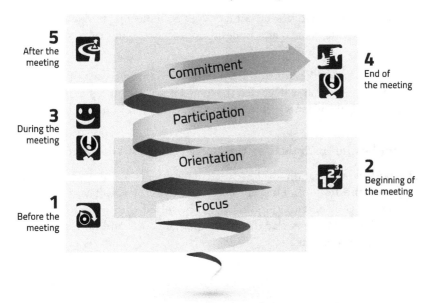

Figure 9 Nudging approaches for the four Meet-Up cornerstones over time

This table and spiral graphic are still relatively abstract and cannot yet be applied directly. Although the table systematically shows the root causes of the meeting misery and the spiral chart illustrates the corresponding solution approaches, how can this be implemented in a specific way?

↓ We recommend four ways you can use the Meet-Up model:

> As an *evaluation* for the current state of your meetings, you can use the four cornerstones already outlined. In this chapter, you will find a quick and straightforward self-test, including an evaluation of the need for action.

> As a *checklist* or reminder for the key success factors of a meeting. You will also find the checklist in this chapter (as well as on our website www.meetup-book.com as a PDF template).

> As a *map* or table of contents for the nudging ideas in this book. To this end, we will show you a nudge overview radar in this chapter – a kind of top-down view of the meeting spiral. You can see to which factor a nudge belongs and what its functional principle is.

> As a *design plan* for the creation of your own meeting nudges. You can use the phases, areas and nudging approaches to improve your meetings in a new way.

We would now like to introduce you briefly to the four ways of using the Meet-Up model. You will see that the model is not merely a theory and can provide tangible benefits – from diagnostic tools to solution aids.

Application 1: Evaluating the Current State of Your Meetings

One possible application for the Meet-Up model – as mentioned – is to use it as a diagnostic tool. This can help you decide if you have a meeting problem in your organisation that could be solved with nudging. Simply answer the following twelve questions spontaneously and honestly *before* reading the evaluation.

Questions about Focus

1 Rarely	2 Now and then	3 Frequently	4 Constantly

1. Does your organisation or department have *too many meetings*? In other words, are there meetings to which you are invited but seem unnecessary?

2. Do discussions in meetings diverge from key the points? Are there any *side issues* that take up too much time?

3. Are meetings you attend overloaded with items so you can't cover them all?

Questions about Orientation

4. Do you feel as if you're *talking at cross purposes* in meetings, for example, when someone is already suggesting ideas while others are still defining the problem?

5. Do you know from your own experience meetings where matters of no interest or relevance to the majority of participants are discussed at length?

6. In the meetings you attend, do conversations go around in circles? Do people jump back and forth between problem definition, solution ideas and clarification?

Questions about Involvement

7. Do certain individuals dominate your meetings (e.g. the boss or an expert)?

8. Do you think that shy or introverted colleagues have difficulty participating in meetings?

9. Do you get the impression that expertise or specialist knowledge is not sufficiently shared in meetings?

Questions about Commitment

10. Have you experienced a situation in which previously assigned tasks had to be re-delegated in subsequent meetings because responsibility for them was still unclear?

11. Do you feel that colleagues in meetings try to avoid accepting responsibility for tasks?

12. Do your meetings explicitly check which measures adopted at the last meeting have been implemented or what their current status is? [N.B. The possible answers to this question are in reverse order.]

Evaluation:
Now add up the numbers (above your answers) and compare the total with the evaluation below.

12–24 points:
'Those who cease to be better have ceased to be good.'
Your meeting culture already seems to be very professional. Typical meeting problems affect you less than other organisations. However, research shows that *leaders/chairpersons often overestimate the productivity of their own meetings.*

→ Ask your colleagues whether they share your optimistic view. Keep what works well and add appropriate nudges and methods from this book to your toolbox.

25–33 points:
'Take the next step.'

You suffer from typical meeting problems in your organisation. This does not mean that meetings are the main problem in your organisation, but you should try – at least in your area of influence – to improve the quality of your meetings.

→ To do this, focus on a few elements and standards and try to use or maintain them consistently (e.g. a permanently visible meeting agenda). The nudges in this book will help you establish new, productive meeting practices.

More than 33 points:
'Urgent need for action.'

Alarm bells! Your meeting problem has reached threatening proportions and you need to do something about it quickly. A large number of issues are likely to have a negative impact on employee satisfaction in your organisation or organisational unit.

→ Find like-minded people who recognise the problem and lead the way as good role models. Test your favourite nudges from the Meet-Up book and your colleagues' responses. If possible, quickly expand the use of meeting practices that have been met with high levels of acceptance in your workplace.

Besides this unique analysis of your Meet-Up maturity level, it can also be useful to improve the quality of individual meetings and avoid pitfalls. Another application of the Meet-Up model is a checklist, which you can also find online at www.meetup-book.com.

Application 2: Checklist before the Start of the Meeting

Just like airline pilots, you can use the Meet-Up checklist before the start of a meeting to ensure the essential success factors. Beforehand, go through the following points and indicate whether each element is a 'yes' or a 'not really'. If you are not usually chairing the meeting yourself, you can also leave this checklist on the meeting table (for others or your colleagues) or give it to a colleague as a useful tool.

For each of the following statements, please select whether it is either "relevant for the meeting" or "rather not relevant for the meeting".

	Yes	Not really
Focus	☐	☐
Orientation	☐	☐
Involvement	☐	☐
Commitment	☐	☐

Focus

The topic needs to be discussed (no alternatives are possible).
All the people attending are necessary for this meeting.
The focus of the meeting is clearly defined and ring-fenced.
The number of sub-items can be discussed within the scheduled time.

Orientation

The sequence of agenda items makes sense (overview-details-review-planning).
The duration of the individual items corresponds to the interests/needs of the participants.
Participants have been given sufficient information.

Involvement

Interactive elements make up a large part of the meeting.
Introverted or new members have the opportunity to get involved quickly and discreetly.
Frequent speakers are not given many opportunities to dominate the meeting.
There is space for informal exchanges and humour.

Commitment

I have allocated time at the end to discuss the allocation of tasks.
I can check the fulfilment of tasks in a subsequent meeting.
I can ensure that tasks are allocated fairly among participants.
If you have answered 'not really' to more than two elements before a meeting, you should, whenever possible, reconsider the shape of your meeting and adapt it accordingly. Pay particular attention to our suggestions in Chapters 5–8 of this book.

By the way, we strongly advise you not to hand over such a 'list of shortcomings' to the chairperson at the end of a meeting. Remember the relationship aspect of each meeting and that giving negative feedback needs a delicate touch.

Application 3: A Map of the Meeting Nudges in This Book

↑ The core innovation in this book is applying the nudging approach to make meetings more productive. Therefore, we need to make it as easy as possible for you to find your best nudges and to provide a comprehensive overview that is as informative as possible (see Figure 10). The nudges are

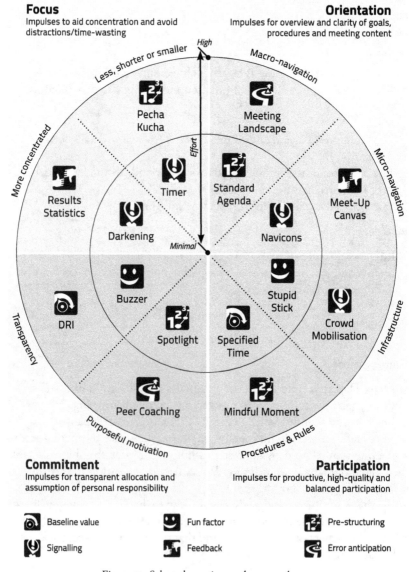

Figure 10 Selected meeting nudges at a glance

assigned to the four cornerstones already mentioned and the closer to the centre of the circle the nudge lies, the less effort we think you will need to implement it. The symbol next to each nudge indicates the principle by which it works.

Application 4: Creating Your Own Meeting Nudges

If you are not content with trying out our ready-made nudges and want to create some of your own, our simple model will help you. You can use the five meeting *phases*, four *cornerstones* and six nudging *principles* to improve meetings in exciting new ways. The meeting phase refers to the 'when' of the nudge or its time of application, the cornerstones are the 'what for' or goal, and the nudging principle the 'how' (i.e. its mode of action).

→ So how do you begin to create meeting nudges yourself and determine their 'when', 'for what' and 'how'? We recommend that you use our meeting Nudge Designer, which allows you to create your nudge in nine steps.

Below you will find a detailed description of each step for creating your own nudges:

1. **Diagnosis:** First, determine the most significant shortcomings at your current meetings. You can use the self-test or the checklist from earlier. Make a note of the Meet-Up cornerstone causing the problem – focus, orientation, involvement or commitment? The outcome of this step is identifying a specific meeting problem that you want to solve (e.g. chronic delays getting started, minimum involvement, no one does what has been agreed, etc.).

2. **Target definition:** Next, determine the 'what for' or goal you want to achieve. What specific behaviour would you like to promote or discourage? Think about how participants have acted before (without the nudge) and how you want them to act after the nudge. Record your ideas in the corresponding sections of the meeting Nudge Designer (see Figure 11). For example, do you want to encourage punctuality, good discussion or better meeting preparation and follow-up?

3. **Time of application:** Now consider when your nudge should ideally take effect. Specify the phase in which it is to be applied. To promote punctuality, you could, for example, place a timer on the table at the

beginning of a meeting or simply say that after 30 minutes a guest will join the group to listen to the findings.

4. **Developing options:** Once you have decided on the 'what for' and the 'when', it is time to choose the right nudging approach. You should also consider the context of your meetings, i.e. infrastructure (in the meeting room), personalities involved, corporate culture, etc. For example, the fun-factor approach to sensitive topics or with highly sceptical people can be harder than nudges about pre-structuring or default values. Hierarchy and leadership style must also be taken into account when developing a nudge; this is especially important with feedback nudges because not every manager can easily handle direct feedback about their meeting style. At this stage, consider whether your nudge should affect the group as a whole or just individuals.

Don't worry, in Chapters 5–8 you will be introduced to a whole range of nudges from which you can learn and get inspiration. The Nudge Designer allows you to develop ideas for all six nudging approaches. Before you go into the details, compare your ideas with

Meeting Nudge Designer

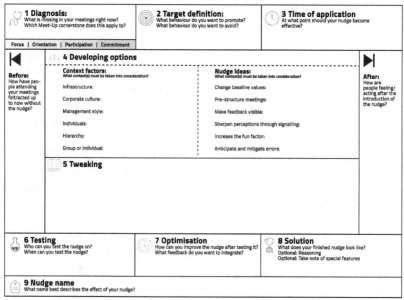

Figure 11 The meeting nudge designer for creating your own impulses

the notes on context. Decide on a nudge which you work out in detail in the next stage.

5. **Tweaking:** Now it's time for the implementation of the nudge. Depending on the situation, this can be done with minimal effort, or it may require some spatial changes.

6. **Testing:** Test your meeting nudge on a small group of teammates before going to other departments or meetings with customers. In this way, you can be sure that the impulse will achieve its desired effect and not be misinterpreted.

7. **Optimisation and routinisation:** If the nudge has proven its worth, you can use it in other meeting contexts, recommend it to other colleagues and possibly even write about it to encourage others to try it. If you receive feedback about the nudge in practice, this can be integrated into the optimisation of the nudge.

8. **Solution:** After you have worked out, tested, and optimised your nudge, it is time to note down how the nudge solves the problem you defined initially. Alternatively, you can write down a short reason for your choice of nudge and what special features you and other nudge-users should consider.

9. **Nudge name:** Finally, you should give your nudge a name to make it easier for you and others to recall, integrate it into your context and use it in the future.

To make these development stages easier for you, we have provided a meeting Nudge Designer here in this book and on our website. With this template, you can design nudge prototypes and quickly structure and improve your idea.

In the following example, we have structured a nudge developed by us based on this template. It addresses the well-known problem of meetings taking up a lot of time that can't be used any other way. This is annoying for those present and leaves little time for meaningful exchanges. We want to help prevent this with an involvement impulse. Figure 12 shows the Nudge Designer being applied to this very problem.

Before you start designing your own nudges, take a look at the sample nudges in the following chapters. Then decide if these are sufficient for your particular needs right now or whether you need to take matters into your own hands.

As inspiration for your own nudges and true to the visualisation motto 'Overview first, then details-on-demand' (from Ben Shneiderman [1996]), Figure 13 gives you an overview of all 100 nudges in this book, divided into

Meeting Nudge Designer

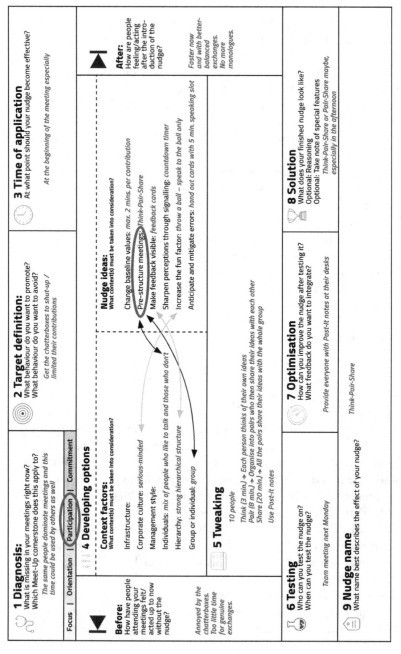

Figure 12 Example of a completed Meeting Nudge Designer

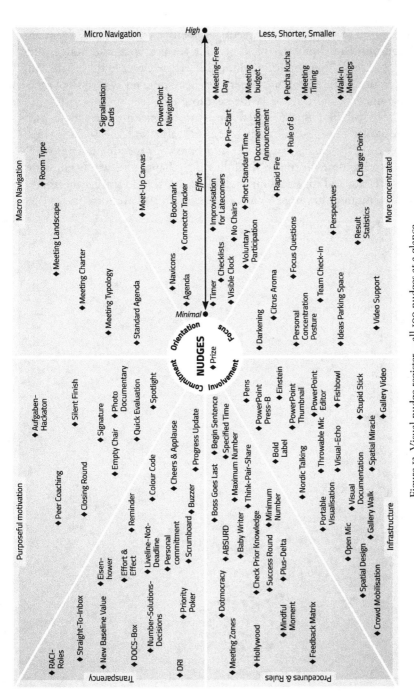

Figure 13 Visual nudge register – all 100 nudges at a glance

the four cornerstones for better meetings – focus, orientation, involvement and commitment. For each of these four cornerstones, the nudges are arranged so that those requiring minimal effort are closer to the centre and those requiring more effort are closer to the circumference. Details of each of these nudges can be found in the next four chapters.

→ You will find this overview in a printer-friendly format on our website (www.meetup-book.com). You will also find the tools in this Chapter as PDF templates and you can share your meeting nudges with others in the online forum. In the following Chapter, we will begin with the focus factor and suggest some nudges for shorter and smaller meetings, as well as impulses for more better concentration and productivity.

CHAPTER 5

Focus

Concentrating on the Right Thing

← Imagine the following situation we found ourselves in recently:

> You are on the management floor of a large infrastructure office. The huge conference table is made of beautiful wood with recessed retractable monitors. On the walls hang expensive paintings and a huge plasma screen. The espresso is excellent. An hour-long meeting with the Board of Directors on the topic of strategy adjustment has been scheduled, and only four of the twelve expected attendees have arrived. Fifteen minutes later, the meeting is now underway but key people keep leaving the room to make phone calls. Instead of discussing strategy, those present talk about where they live, problems with the computer network and politics. You stare at the scene in disbelief for a while and then courageously ask about the reasons for a strategy adjustment. Almost immediately, you regret speaking up because it gives rise to a 15-minute monologue by the Chairman, beginning with strategy but then digressing into regulatory frameworks. It seems like the CEO has hit a nerve because people are starting to agree with him and sharing other (partly personal) anecdotes about problems with local authorities. Two minutes before the scheduled end of the meeting, you are asked if you have any further questions and, if not, are ready to support the strategy adjustment. What do you do?

To put this into context, the meeting described took place in southern Europe and the observer is from the north. In this case, he politely declined to support the strategy because such an array of focusing problems is rare even for a south European country. To a lesser extent, however, we have also experienced similar situations in Germany, Austria, Switzerland, France and the United States, with meetings not starting punctually, lacking clear management of expectations regarding goals and procedures, and far too many participants for a helpful or productive discussion.

And instead of concentrating on the matters in hand, the session descends into a chaotic collection of mini-meetings or backbiting exchanges.

↑ In this chapter, you will find a wealth of simple impulses for holding *fewer* meetings, *shortening* and *reducing* meetings (in terms of participant numbers) and boosting *concentration* in meetings. In other words, it's about focusing on *time*, *people* and *issues*. Mostly, we will use the nudging principles of pre-structuring and default values, but we can also bring in the fun factor and signalling for better focus. This increases the quality of meetings and considerably reduces the time they take.

You will see that *reasonable restriction* is one of the best opportunities for focusing. You can make such restrictions relatively easy by specifying new default values or by pre-structuring. But there are also playful possibilities. We'll show you these with the help of the following nudges for fewer meetings, shorter meetings, smaller meetings and – in particular – more focused meetings.

Nudges for Fewer Meetings

The solution to the 'meeting problem' begins with the question of when you should hold a meeting at all.

Some people think the best meetings are those that never happen, but we disagree. We believe in the enormous potential that is released by groups thinking together in a goal-oriented way. However, we are not suggesting that you cancel all regular meetings immediately and only hold those that are absolutely necessary – even though some companies have done just that.

The fact remains, however, that many meetings are unnecessary and could be easily replaced by a series of e-mails or short telephone calls. Not every topic is suitable for a meeting context – think, for example, of highly sensitive or complex matters better suited for a small group or workshop.

But what criteria should be used to decide for or against a meeting?

→ Our first impulse for 'calling a meeting' is a simple **Checklist** and this answers this question. This pre-structuring is a nudge to hold only necessary meetings and, ideally, this short checklist would appear automatically on the screen as an IT nudge when you invite colleagues to a meeting.

If more questions are answered 'mainly no' rather than 'mainly yes', you should probably refrain from calling a meeting.

Do you really need a meeting? A decision-oriented checklist

Questions	Mainly yes	Mainly no
1. The topic concerns a relatively large number of people.	☐	☐
2. A lot has happened since the last meeting in this circle.	☐	☐
3. The topic requires a number of perspectives and expert input.	☐	☐
4. The information requires a great deal of explanation and cannot simply be mailed.	☐	☐
5. Stakeholder involvement in the issue is essential.	☐	☐
6. It is important for everyone to meet again (or get to know each other) and exchange ideas.	☐	☐
7. It is important to be able to 'sell' the topic on a personal level.	☐	☐
8. In the meeting, people can learn vital facts that go beyond the intake of information.	☐	☐
9. There will be many questions being answered clearly during the meeting.	☐	☐
10. There is no other suitable format for the information and concerns (e.g. sending information by e-mail, recording video messages, one-on-one conversations, etc.).	☐	☐
11. It is practical to bring critical decision-makers and experts together at this meeting.	☐	☐
12. The information necessary to discuss the topic properly is already available and has been distributed.	☐	☐

In this case, an appropriate IT system would advise you not to have a meeting but to postpone it and invite fewer people. This decentralised impulse can encourage many people to reconsider the necessity of a meeting, relieving pressure on colleagues.

A much stricter nudge to promote fewer meetings consists of having a **Meeting-Free Day** or at least one morning. To protect employee productivity, it is made generally known that Wednesdays, for example, are free from meetings (in principle). Mondays and Fridays seem less suitable as they could be used for covert extended weekends.

Organisations such as Hewlett Packard or the European Central Bank have experimented with this impulse. However, it is more about fighting symptoms than eliminating the underlying problem, namely that there are too many unnecessary or poorly prepared meetings in the first place. A moratorium on meetings for a limited period can draw attention to the 'meeting proliferation problem'. However, this can also lead to coordination problems and time bottlenecks, especially with highly mobile teams.

Remember that a nudge is almost always based on freedom of choice. However, department heads may choose to overrule an agreed ban on meetings if they consider it necessary and, in our experience, this happens all too frequently. A final – somewhat daring and extremely centralist – nudge for reducing the number of meetings is the **Meeting Budget**. Each team receives an allowance of five meeting hours per month. If these team meeting hours are used up, all further team meeting attendance is voluntary. This means that team leaders approach the issue of meetings more carefully and strive to make the most of existing schedules.

The problem of the number of meetings is, of course, mitigated to a certain extent if every single meeting takes less time, and this is precisely what we are looking at in the following section.

Nudges for Shorter Meetings

Many of us complain about an endless stream of meetings, but wouldn't it be fantastic if we could also use nudges to make them shorter? The great news is that such nudges already exist and many of them are easy to implement. Placing a clearly **Visible Clock** helps, for example, to improve time discipline. Unfortunately, this simple aid is still missing in many meeting rooms. Google has modernised this nudge somewhat, and in many of their meeting rooms, a second beamer projects the remaining time in real-time using a countdown **Timer**. A cheaper version of this nudge consists of placing a simple hourglass (egg timer) on the meeting table. The passing of time is visible to all, stimulating focus and goal orientation.

Removing the chairs from the meeting room (or simply moving them to the side) is another easy-to-use impulse for shorter meetings that also increases participant commitment. In IT project management, people speak of **Stand Up** meetings, which take place within the framework of techniques such as *scrum* or *agile* in organisations.

In stand-up meetings, employees stand in front of a large whiteboard every morning while the tasks for the day are discussed in just 15–20 minutes. At Immobilienscout24 in Berlin, they don't even need a meeting room for this because the meetings take place standing in the corridor in front of the project board.

Even a carefully chosen **Meeting Time** can help to reduce the overrun of the meeting time. To do this, schedule a meeting directly before the 1 pm lunch break (e.g. starting at 12:15 pm).

One of the strongest nudges for a shorter meeting duration is a change in the **Standard Time** for meetings. Change the accepted length of meetings in your organisation or at least in your team. In many companies, this is predefined mentally or even by IT systems as one hour. Change this to *half an hour*. One approach that has worked for us is what we call the 5+30 formula. Invite your colleagues to come and have a cup of coffee five minutes before the start of the formal meeting – a kind of **Pre-Start** – so that key issues can be discussed informally and you don't have to start from cold (incidentally, there's an exciting study on this by Mirivel & Tracy, 2005). In return, you agree to end the meeting after 30 minutes.

A five-minute warm-up can work wonders. You can display information on the flipchart in advance, answer questions on an ad-hoc basis and find out what has already been done. This approach also saves time because fewer participants are late and you can start together on time. No Meet-Up without a warm-up could become a simple nudging rule.

Speaking of arriving late, some particularly creative organisations try to reduce this annoying phenomenon by requiring people who come late to do some form of (preferably embarrassing) **Improvisation** as a forfeit. In fact, we have witnessed senior managers who, because they arrived late, had to perform push-ups, sing a song or leap like a ballet dancer – experiences most people would prefer to avoid. So next time, they make a special effort to be punctual. The best nudge of all, of course, is the punctual manager acting as a role model.

What other impulses are there to make meetings shorter? Some partici-pants suffer from 'verbal diarrhea' and – as mentioned at the beginning of this chapter – prolong meetings with digressive monologues. To reduce this tendency, we recommend the **Rapid Fire** method. In this fast-paced round, each person may only make a short statement such as voicing a simple statement or concern about the issue under discussion. This has the pleasant side effect of giving introverted colleagues the obligation to speak as well. Rapid-fire rounds work well for meetings with up to twelve participants, but in larger groups, they may become too lengthy and overtax everyone's attention span. In rapid-fire rounds, by the way, it is best if the most senior (hierarchically) person present has the last word. Otherwise, there is a risk that further contributions will parrot what the boss has said and other essential matters not be raised.

Another way to tame the verbose speaker in presentation situations is **Pecha Kucha**. With a Pecha Kucha presentation, you force yourself and your colleagues to limit their input to 20 slides, each slide remaining visible for only 20 seconds. With these fixed guidelines, you help yourself and others to focus on the essentials and present them in a strictly defined 6 minutes and 40 seconds. The days of never-ending presentations may finally come to an end.

However, it is a challenge for every participant to bring their content to a fixed format of 20 slides and to coordinate their presentations in such a way that each slide is changed after 20 seconds. The advantage is that you can do this easily with PowerPoint.

→ You will find a presentation template with the correct timing at www .meetup-book.com

But even with such a template, Pecha Kucha needs frequent repetition and practice so that the presentation can be kept fluent in the given time. In particular, the transition between slides must be just right or Pecha Kucha can quickly appear confusing or excessively hectic.

← Pecha Kucha dates back to the year 2003. Japanese architects invented this special presentation format at the time to make their exchange of projects and innovations efficient and entertaining at so-called Pecha Kucha nights. The compressed presentation format is currently enjoying great popularity and is now used not only in architecture, but in all areas of life. The pechakucha.org website gives you an overview of public Pecha Kucha presentation evenings around the world. In contrast to business meeting attendees, it suggests 'the more, the merrier'. However, this cannot apply to meetings in organisations because the more participants a meeting has, the more inefficient (and less interactive) it usually becomes. That is why we are now going to look at nudges to reduce the number of session participants.

Nudges for Smaller Meetings

A newly appointed senior manager was confronted by a meeting of almost twenty people. Instead of going straight into the agenda, she asked the person sitting next to her why she was there. The answer ('The fourth item on the agenda might be relevant to our department') did not satisfy the manager, so she politely asked that person to leave and obtain the information elsewhere. Then she turned to the next person with the same question. Again, she didn't think that person's presence was necessary either and it was suggested the results could be e-mailed after the meeting. As she began to question the third person, six other people got up voluntarily and left the meeting room. This is certainly an extreme and somewhat confrontational approach to reducing the size of meetings.

In this case, however, it worked because all future interdepartmental meetings with this manager now took place on a smaller scale thanks to this deterrent nudge.

However, there are also gentler and more diplomatic ways to reduce the size of meetings. Think of the meeting invitation, for example. When announcing a meeting, indicate that all the results and information will be e-mailed after the session, so attendance is not absolutely necessary. This can be helpful because only the really interested and motivated colleagues need become directly involved. At Google, a **Rule of 8** dictates that meetings should not include more than eight people. If more than eight colleagues are interested in attending, they should bring in their concerns via a colleague who can then also inform them about the results.

← At this point, a small pause for reflection. Why do meetings become large so quickly when we know they're unproductive? There are a number of understandable reasons for this. After all, the aim is to consult as many people as possible, to inform as widely as possible and to ensure that colleagues feel included. People want to talk about their work, report with pride about what they have achieved and perhaps secretly seek some recognition for their efforts. Inviting someone to a meeting may also be a way of showing professional respect.

However, all this can also be done without mass meetings but, for example, a bilateral meeting over coffee, a short telephone call or an informative e-mail. Or it can be achieved through new approaches to meetings, such as **Walk-In Walk-Out**, which we will now introduce you to.

→ Another way to keep meetings small is the Walk-In Walk-Out meeting. Some participants only come for the agenda items that are relevant to them. A welcome side effect is that 'time boxing' for each agenda item must be strictly adhered to or starting times will be out of sync. In our experience, however, this type of meeting can also be unsettling for the core group. A more moderate version of this approach would be to invite experts to come and give short presentations during the meeting but leave immediately afterwards.

Inviting someone to join you midway also helps with time discipline ('We have to hurry up now because in 10 minutes Shelagh will be joining us').

Even if large meetings are not very productive, remember that perspective diversity is essential for some issues. However, this potential strength will only work if everyone is really focused on the topic, which brings us to what is probably the most crucial point – the concentration factor in meetings. By this, we mean conducting conversations in a topic-centred, constructive way, without major distractions.

Nudges for Better Concentration in Meetings

You must have attended meetings in which your colleagues – or even you – have read e-mails or studied other documents (for more about this, see Volkema & Neiderman, 1995). You have probably been in sessions where the discussion has drifted to side issues or someone has taken the opportunity to vent their frustration.

How can everyone stay focused on key issues and avoid being side-tracked? To this end, we have ten nudges for you – from the conventional and straightforward to the relatively bold (other interesting impulses are also suggested in Goleman, 2015).

→ The simplest focus impulse to offer consists of **Focus Questions**. These help everyone (in a diplomatic way) to find to return to the main issue and to focus. Here is a selection of our favourite focus questions (even more can be found in Spradley, 2016).

Focus Questions for Meetings

> Is this central to our current topic?
> Does this affect our current problem?
> Should we use our shared meeting time to deal with this now or would it be more productive to clarify this bilaterally afterwards?
> Aren't there more general points we should discuss first?
> I don't understand how this relates to what we're discussing now. Can anyone help me?
> Is it clear to everyone why we are discussing this now? I'm confused.
> Should we really immerse ourselves in these details before we have clarified the overall context?
> Are we ready to move on to the next item now?

With questions like these, you are giving your colleagues and, above all, the person leading the meeting some subtle but valuable feedback, namely that they are running the risk of losing the thread or that the conversation is going off-topic.

Another type of feedback nudge for greater concentration is to keep a record of how many problems you have solved in the meeting, how many decisions you have made, or how many useful ideas have been developed. If you note down these **Results Statistics** on a flipchart from the outset, but it remains empty, this creates visible pressure to proceed constructively and quickly. By the way, we know of a CEO who insists on receiving the results statistics from every single company meeting!

To aid concentration, we have already hinted at some more extreme nudges. Here's one of those. In a windowless meeting room, put all the **Lights Out** for a few minutes and ask everyone to concentrate fully on participant contributions (of course, their computers and mobile phones must be switched off too). If this impulse is too risky for you, here is another tried-and-tested concentration-promoting nudge. Spray a **Citrus Aroma** in the meeting room – but don't overdo it.

Another clever nudge for better concentration that Google uses extensively is to place a mobile phone **Charge Point** at the entrance to the meeting room and ask everyone to use it. This elegantly eliminates the irresistible distraction of a mobile phone.

If these impulses all seem too radical, we have two simple nudges for you.

Practise a **Team Check-In** at the beginning of your session like aircraft crews do. During the first five minutes of the meeting, everyone should briefly and concisely say what is on their minds, what their main concerns for the session are, or what they would like to share with others. This ensures that the meeting can be held in a more focused way afterwards. Let people get things off their chests beforehand so that the meeting can then progress smoothly. Team check-ins can easily take place in the rapid-fire mode mentioned earlier. A more structured form of the Team Check-In nudge can be done using the **Perspectives Method** (Figure 14). Introductory comments can be divided into *questions (?), relevant information or hints (!), challenges/concerns (–) and successes or good news (+)* and recorded by keyword or adhesive card.

You can also use the same template as a **Parking Space** for subsequent questions, hints or problems. This helps to keep the discussion focused while making everyone's concerns clearly visible.

Don't forget to photograph the template at the end of the meeting and attach it to the minutes if necessary.

If you are still having meetings over the phone (although there is no longer any justification for this), here is a valuable tip for focusing during *telephone conferences*. Whenever possible, activate any **Video Support** feature – because video conferencing helps you concentrate. According

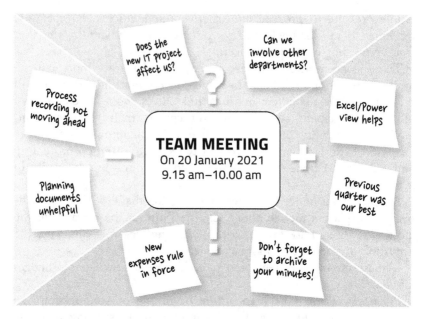

Figure 14 Examples of check-ins using the Perspectives nudge

to a study by Verizon, only 4 per cent of video participants try to multitask, while for telephone conferences this rises to 57 per cent!

Of course, concentrating on the conversation in telephone conferences also helps considerably if you activate your microphone mute while you are not speaking. This will eliminate annoying background noise.

Whether at telephone conferences, team sessions or departmental events, the core resource for focused meetings is your undivided attention. Box 3 tells you how you can maintain this even for long periods.

One more hint at the end of this chapter about focusing. Be attentive and sensitive when it comes to maintaining focus in a group. We know from experience that deviations from the central theme can sometimes be helpful because they lead to new perspectives or ideas. Not every unfocused discussion is automatically wrong. An important indicator of 'useful digression' is whether the debate is constructive and involved, or destructive in the sense of a catalogue of complaints. Pay attention to the facial expressions and gestures of your colleagues. If you see that the side issue sparks positivity and enthusiasm, then perhaps you should allow it to develop for a few minutes. If, however, the laptop screens go up and mobile phones come out, it is essential to return to the main issue without delay.

↓ **Box 3 – How to Concentrate Better in Meetings**

If you find it difficult to stay focused in meetings from time to time, here are five simple tips.

1. **Doodle**. Recent research shows that doodling can increase your concentration and even help you listen (https://tinyurl.com/lmaygfn). Let yourself be inspired by what has been said.
2. Another trick is to **summarise** what has just been said and propose the next practical step.
3. Observe the **reactions** (including facial expressions) of your colleagues to what has been said.
4. Do not mentally end the sentences of your colleagues but try to listen with an open mind and **ask questions** if you don't understand.
5. Pay attention to your **Posture**. Sit upright with your hands on your thighs. Reflect on your own (mental) attitude towards what has been discussed. If it bores or irritates you, consider what you can learn from it.

PS: It would be ironic if, in a chapter about focusing, we were to recommend that you try out everything you have just read. Choose a nudge that you will always use from now on and maybe two more that you will try. As a kind of nudge to self-commitment, there is a list and checkbox at the end of this and the next following chapters.

Focus is *the* single most significant factor for successful meetings. Don't leave this to chance, but consistently (re)focus your meetings through nudging. Try it out, whether through reduced meeting times, simple focus questions or interactive methods such as the rapid-fire round. The table at the very end of this chapter gives you an overview of all focus nudges that you can go ahead with and try them out.

Focus Nudges at a Glance

Which Ones Would You Spontaneously Choose?

	Nudge	Nudging principle	Yes, from now on	I'll try it out	Maybe later
Fewer meetings	Checklist	Pre-structuring	O	O	O
	Meeting Free Day	Default value	O	O	O
	Meeting Budget	Default value	O	O	O
Shorter meetings	Visible Clock	Signalling	O	O	O
	Timer	Signalling	O	O	O
	Stand Up (No chairs)	Pre-structuring	O	O	O
	Meeting Time (just before lunch?)	Mistake anticipation	O	O	O
	(Shorter) Standard Time	New default values	O	O	O
	Pre-Start	Pre-structuring	O	O	O
	Improvisation	Fun factor	O	O	O
	Rapid Fire	Pre-structuring	O	O	O
	Pecha Kucha	Pre-structuring	O	O	O
Smaller meetings	Rule of 8	Default value	O	O	O
	Walk-In Walk-Out	Default value	O	O	O
More concentration	Focus Questions	Mistake anticipation	O	O	O
	Results Statistics	Feedback	O	O	O
	Citrus Aroma	Signalling	O	O	O
	Lights Out	Signalling	O	O	O
	Team Check-In	Pre-structuring	O	O	O
	Charge Point	Pre-structuring	O	O	O
	Perspectives Method	Pre-structuring	O	O	O
	Parking Space	Mistake anticipation	O	O	O
	Video Support	Signalling	O	O	O
	Posture	Signalling	O	O	O

CHAPTER 6

Orientation
A Navigator for Meetings

← One of the best meetings we ever attended as moderators enabled a diagnostics company to bring its latest product to market six months earlier than planned, generating significant additional revenue. How was this achieved?

Believe it or not, the breakthrough came about because we were able to create and maintain *orientation* in a critical discussion despite an incredible amount of detail. Thanks to skilful navigation through the various issues (technical, medical, legal and commercial), the team was able to gain remarkable new insights and remove several go-to-market barriers more quickly than expected.

Practically speaking, this took place in a so-called 'lessons learned meeting', when past mistakes, successes and their consequences (findings and measures taken) are jointly considered. The following illustration (Figure 15) shows the poster we used.

The *type of meeting* (in this case, a retrospective session) was also crucial for the orientation and actions of the participants since it led to a learner-oriented attitude. In this case, it was about the experience gained during the development of a new measuring instrument.

Up to that point, the German, Swiss and American engineers and managers involved had already discussed such things in (monthly) meetings, but often became sidetracked, dug their heels in, talked over each other or (even worse) conducted witch-hunts – instead of learning together from the past and converting findings into action.

What was so different about this meeting? Actually, it was simply that we used a lot of *orientation aids*. From the start, we clearly designated this a lessons-learned meeting and then visualised the entire development process, using it as a point of reference whenever individual experiences were discussed. We categorised each comment about the past with corresponding pin cards either as a success (and started with it), a failure, an insight, or an action required. We signalled to the group whether they were

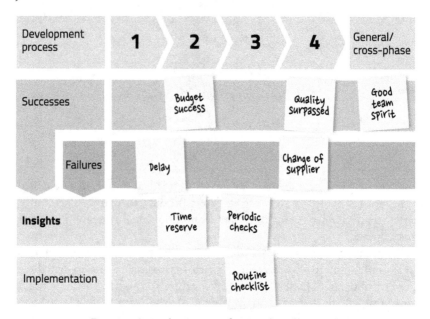

Figure 15 A visual orientation for recording experiences

in the middle of an overview discussion or a detailed discussion, and we set them relatively strict time limits.

Simple *signal or communication cards* helped the team to see whether they were talking about what had already happened or what was necessary for the future as well as whether they wanted to go into the details of a success or a failure – or rather discuss the situation in overview mode.

↓ During this session, the Americans involved even went so far (too far in our opinion, but it didn't harm the atmosphere) to design and immediately use signal cards for when they were being humorous. Since the American engineers and managers repeatedly used irony, which the German and Swiss participants interpreted as a serious contribution, the Americans quickly designed two more signal cards. One said, 'Joke!' the other said, 'No joke!'

You don't have to go to such extremes with a signalling nudge, but a little push to show everyone you are trying to lighten the mood can do wonders for productivity. That is what this chapter is about – staying on course in meetings, avoiding confusion and not talking at cross-purposes.

Of course, signal cards are not the only way, but they are the most obvious.

↑ In this chapter, you will learn about different impulses that help control the often-complicated flow of conversations during meetings, how to navigate through multi-issue meetings and how to plan the phases of a meeting.

→ For this purpose, we will now introduce you to a simple but unusual tool that helps steer a course through complex discussions – the *Navicon*. Navicons consist of four simple graphic signs that clearly signal to all participants what kind of conversation they are having or about to have. You will have come across these already at the beginning of the book as a reader guidance aid. Navicons also offer orientation because their place-ment on a poster, flipchart or presentation slide means that you can immediately see what everyone wants to discuss and in what form. You can also use Navicons as a form of voting in meetings. When preparing for a meeting, Navicons also help determine the correct order for discussion topics. You can see these little miracle tools for better meetings and their meanings in Figure 16. The bookmark you received with this publication can also be used as a Navicon – simply place it on the meeting table and rotate it in keeping with the current discussion. You can use it as a request

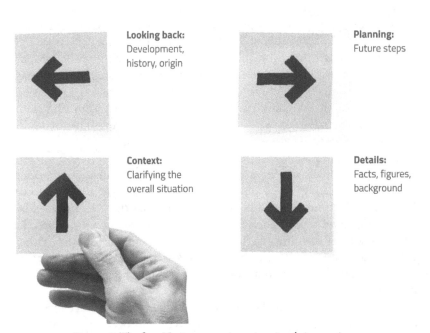

Figure 16 The four Navicons as orientation signals in meetings

to change the direction of the conversation by holding it up accordingly. Alternatively, you can place it on the flipchart next to an essential item.

↑ While these Navicon symbols are there for navigation within a meeting, this chapter also introduces you to ways in which you can create orientation through a series of meetings rather than just individual ones. To do this, we need to distinguish between two levels of meeting navigation – *the macro* and the *micro level*.

The macro level deals with the question of what type of meeting to hold (when and how) while the micro level addresses the individual phases (and discussion parts) of a meeting. For both areas, we will introduce you to various practical nudges from feedback to signals. So let's get going and start with the macro level, that is, those nudges that provide orientation through many different meetings.

Macro Navigation: Orientation beyond the Individual Meeting

→ In our research on meeting productivity, we have looked at organisations from small businesses to large government agencies and observed many different meeting formats. An initial nudge to take control of the situation is to give the organisation concerned clear feedback about what meetings are a burden on its employees and to signal which meetings are necessary – and which are not. To do this, we use a simple format we call a **Meeting Landscape**. All regular meetings are entered into one of four columns. You start on the left with daily meetings, then enter weekly meetings, and finally monthly and quarterly meetings. The longer a session usually lasts, and the more people involved (marked by horizontal or vertical strokes), the higher up you place this meeting. Thanks to its graphical composition, the management team should be able to orient itself and optimise the meeting landscape.

↓ In the example given (Figure 17), the management team saw at a glance that weekly meetings were putting a massive strain on the workforce (the second column is very full) so shortened departmental meetings by integrating some aspects into more compact information meetings. In addition, management meetings were now to be held on a monthly rather than weekly basis. Team check-in sessions were cancelled altogether as people expressed the view that coordination would function better informally and bilaterally.

It was also decided to make attendance at divisional exchange meetings optional. Finally, the quarterly meetings were improved by sending out information two days in advance.

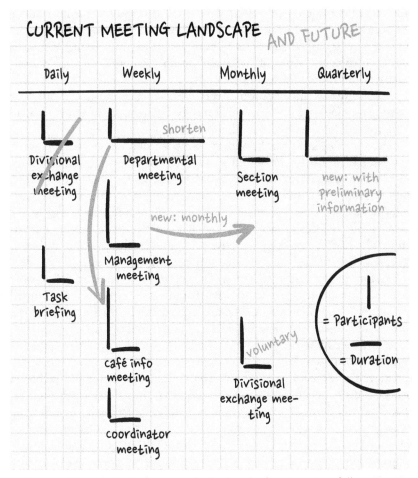

Figure 17 The meeting landscape as a feedback nudge for orientation of all meetings

This nudge is not primarily about reducing the number of meetings (this was covered in Chapter 5, on focusing), but about the optimal coordination of different meeting formats. However, it is a desirable side effect to reduce the overall negative impact of too many meetings.

↓ Depending on how much analysis you want to conduct, it can also be useful to evaluate the individual meetings with Navicons. The minute-taker notes the proportion of detailed discussions, overview discussions, reviews and planning time in each session to identify (positive or negative) patterns and to make the various meeting types more consistent (more on this later under micro navigation). This takes us straight to the next nudge for better orientation in meetings – the **Meeting Typology**. One of the most frequently asked questions by participants in our training sessions is what the different types of meetings are and whether we should limit ourselves to just one format.

Our answer to this question is very clear – there are indeed different meeting typologies (e.g. Allen et al. 2014), but you should invent your own! Also, it is advisable to avoid mixing the styles.

But, one thing at a time. In research, a distinction is often made between *informative, decision-making* and *problem-solving* meetings and meetings with a *training* or *tribute element*. Similarly, there is also the **TIDE** abbreviation for different types of meeting – **T**eam meetings, **I**nformation meetings, **D**iscussion meetings, **E**volvement meetings.

Why is it helpful to label meetings like this? Because people need to know whether they can play an active role, whether they should just listen, whether they should be creative or whether, at the end of the day, a decision will be made together. Therefore, a classification of specific meetings can make sense, as we saw in the case of the 'lessons learned' session earlier. However, in reality, no decision can be reached without the discussion and development of ideas and at the end of creative meetings, decisions are often needed, such as which points need to be pursued further. In our opinion, a good nudge should clearly state the primary function of the meeting (e.g. information event, experience and exchange forum, creative meeting or team coordination), but always with the hint that there will be other aspects. It can be helpful to use an *in-house meeting typology* that is as close as possible to the employees' roles in terms of vocabulary and meeting aims. Even the name of the meeting is a nudge that helps to align those attending with its primary purpose. 3M's meeting typology includes, for example, review or presentation meetings as separate entities.

If you are interested in how meetings are classified, there is an entire dissertation covering this topic, which you can find online here: https://tinyurl.com/yaee34vr

How can you signal the primary purpose of a meeting in a way that is crystal-clear? One trick that numerous companies such as Google, Credit Suisse and Swisscom (the Swiss telecommunications company) use is to have a different **Spatial Design** for each type of meeting. At Swisscom, for example, we deliberately held training sessions in the so-called reframing room. A collection of broken and disassembled picture frames on the walls provided a constant indication that the aim of our sessions was to think

↓ Box 4 – A Brief Typology of Participants

Speaking of typology, in addition to a typology of the main types of meeting, it may also be helpful to visualise the (empirically validated) typology of a meeting's participants and to see how best to deal with them. Professor Kauffeld from the Technical University of Braunschweig in Germany identified the following meeting participants. The table (supplemented by our nudges) by Simone Kauffeld and Verena Güntner comes from the magazine 'OrganisationsEntwicklung' mentioned at the beginning of the book. It shows, among other things, how you can turn persistent moaners into productive participants, e.g. through a form of 'wailing wall' at the start of the meeting.

PARTICIPANT TYPE TYPICAL CONTRIBUTIONS EFFECT MEASURES AND NUDGES

The Complainer

Share: 35%
- Frequent whining and negative comments
- Little interest in change
- Gets lost in details and examples
- Low satisfaction with meetings
- Low success in implementing planned measures
- Show Navicon pointing upwards repeatedly
- Work in pairs instead of the whole group
- Create opportunities for expressing opinions over the entire course of the process
- Individual discussion before the meeting
- Create a 'wailing wall' (see above)

The Dedicated Problem-Solver

Share: 20.7%
- Has a lot of organisational knowledge
- Identifies and explains solutions
- Open to change
- High satisfaction with meetings and overall job satisfaction
- The implementation of planned measures succeeds better
- Pay particular attention when leading the meeting
- Pay attention to his/her constructive feedback
- Activate using right arrow Navicon

The Problem Analyst

Share: 18.8%
- Explains problems
- Describes causes and consequences
- Tends to complain sometimes
- Behaviour can be process-enhancing
- Too many problem analysts are associated with reduced success in implementing measures, high levels of resignation and lower job satisfaction
- Create a 'wailing wall'
- Use the arrow up or forward Navicon to change their perspective

The Uninterested

Share: 17.1%
- Blames and criticises others
- Frequently has side conversations
- Little overall involvement in the discussion
- No influence or can be disruptive
- Increase commitment by creating and strengthening participative elements (e.g. shared leadership or working in pairs)
- Focus on the composition of participants. Only invite people relevant to the discussion

The Moderator

Share: 7.8%
- Summarises results
- Asks questions that encourage progress
- Can distinguish fact from personal opinion
- Meetings become more structured – better orientation in meetings
- Stronger emphasis on the principle of shared leadership
- Use Navicons and signal type of meeting to everyone

differently and break out of the existing framework. It became immediately apparent to everyone that flexibility and a variety of perspectives were in demand. In another Swisscom room, more than a dozen shoes are glued to the wall as a subtle hint to participants to put themselves in the 'shoes of the customer'. Scientifically speaking, such impulses are called 'priming' (i.e. a subtle influence on attitude through existing stimuli), and we have seen these priming nudges before. Do you remember the stuffed animals mentioned at the beginning of the book to promote more constructive discussions? What about research which shows that people in rooms with plants are far more creative than those in places without plants? Figure 18 illustrates further examples of rooms as nudges.

↓ Walt Disney also had different offices for different tasks – a creative one for brainstorming, one filled with drawing tools for putting ideas into practice and an uncluttered one for idea evaluation. Similarly, in some organisations, we have seen meeting rooms that physically signal the primary purpose of a meeting such as project rooms with large horizontal whiteboards for planning, or spaces in which virtual meetings can be held particularly well. In a publishing house, we experienced a creative space for the development of new ideas and in some banks (small, elegantly furnished) meeting rooms for discreet client conferences. The hearing aid manufacturer Sonova even has a meeting room in a genuine sauna – helpful when discussing particularly 'hot' topics!

↑ In addition to the meeting landscape, the meeting typology and customised rooms, there are two other ways of providing orientation beyond the individual meeting – the Meeting Charter and the Standard Agenda. Let's take a brief look at these two macro-orientation nudges before we address orientation in individual meetings.

Figure 18 Broken frames (left) and shoes on the wall (right) as nudges for a change of perspective (Source: Swisscom)

A **Meeting Charter** (or the ground rules) are a set of *regulations* that provide orientation for all meetings. Many teams define some basic standards for conduct in meetings at the beginning of any project. Below are some examples of particularly successful meeting charter entries:

> We get to team meetings on time and start and finish them as scheduled.
> We send the agenda to all participants at least two hours before a meeting and have it visible in the room for all to see.
> We only include people who are directly affected or can contribute something valuable.
> We won't interrupt each other in meetings but let everyone finish talking – unless the following rule is persistently ignored.
> We will be brief and only speak if we can contribute something relevant and constructive.
> The person with the lowest seniority in the room should be allowed to present their ideas first.
> At the end of each meeting, everyone will have the opportunity to say briefly what is particularly important to him or her.
> Each team meeting will be minuted to record the issues discussed and any outstanding decisions or tasks (including clear responsibilities and deadlines).

In some companies we have worked with, these remarks are immortalised on posters or a cube lying on the meeting table, serving as an ever-present nudge. Be careful not to include more than seven or eight entries in your charter and back up their nudge effect with meaningful images or symbols. In the following box are some of the favourite meeting rules of well-known leaders.

Of course, you don't need to be quite so dictatorial to increase the productivity of sessions, which brings us nicely to our final, relatively gentle orientation nudge – the **Standard Agenda** – which can be used for more than one meeting.

The essential tool for orientation in meetings is the (permanently visible and updated) agenda. But what makes a good agenda? What do meaningful meeting plans that can function as orientation nudges for very different meeting formats look like? Fortunately, the literature here has some helpful (and concurring) things to offer. We would like to recommend the following three memorable *'universal agendas'* for your flipchart.

↓ **Box 5 – Meeting Rules of Famous Leaders**

Jeff Bezos (CEO of Amazon) formulated the two-pizza rule – a meeting should not include more people than can be fed with two pizzas.

Bill Gates (founder of Microsoft) insisted on seeing and discussing the 'lowlights' (i.e. failures and current problems), as the first presentation slide at review meetings.

Reinhold Würth, the man behind the success of the German-based fastening and assembly technology giant for many years, recognised that different terms for the same thing are a productivity killer at meetings. For this reason, he decided what expressions would be in worldwide use and integrated them into regular communications. Alternative understandings or use of these terms is not tolerated.

Oprah Winfrey (US talk show host and entrepreneur) usually doesn't hold any meetings at all and prefers bilateral phone calls unless a meeting is unavoidable.

Elon Musk (CEO at Tesla) has an unwritten rule in his meetings – be prepared or prepare to be taken apart in the question round. Another one of his meeting rules is 'no proposal without a factual basis'.

His Holiness, the Dalai Lama, also seems to follow an unwritten rule – no meetings without cheerfulness. Anyone who has met this person (including when he visited us at the University of St. Gallen) will agree that no encounter with him is without humour, joy and positive charisma.

Sheryl Sandberg (COO of Facebook) leads the meeting with a tally sheet. Once all the points have been crossed out, the meeting ends immediately.

Ray Dalio (legendary founder of Bridgewater Associates) made it a rule that practically all meetings were audio-recorded. The result was that employees endeavoured to make only clear and helpful contributions – and then also to implement promised tasks quickly, since everyone could listen back to what they had committed themselves to.

Richard Branson (founder of the Virgin Group) has an inspiring session rule – unconventional ideas require unconventional meeting locations. That's why he tells his managers to hold meetings in the park or in the coffee shop around the corner, especially when new ideas are needed.

Mark Suster (US entrepreneur and investor at Upfront Ventures) has as a rule for most meetings – no open laptops. Laptops lead to inattention and distractions, signalling that you are not interested in the conversation. People are explicitly requested to keep them closed.

Barack Obama had one simple rule at staff meetings – no mobile phones. As a nudge for this, he would place a small basket at the door where all aides had to deposit their mobile phones before a meeting.

The SPIN Agenda:

1. **Situation:** What's it all about today?
2. **Problem:** Why is this generally problematic/important and for whom?
3. **Implications:** What exactly are the causes and consequences of the problem?
4. **Next steps:** Who does what and by when?

The SPIN agenda cleverly varies the different Navicons. First, the situation and the problem are looked at 'upwards' and an overview is possible. Then the implications are looked at 'downwards' and 'backwards', that is, the details and the origin of the problem are discussed. The final stage is to 'look ahead' and plan the next steps.

Universal Meeting Agenda by Axelrod:

1. **Welcome:**
   How can we make a positive start possible for everyone?
2. **Introduce people and tasks:**
   How can we bring everyone together?
3. **Clarify the situation:**
   How can we create curiosity and commitment to the topic?
4. **View options and wishes:**
   Wie mobilisieren wir die Ideen aller?
5. **Define responsibilities:**
   How can we create a fair distribution of tasks?
6. **Find a coherent conclusion:**
   What can we learn from the meeting process?

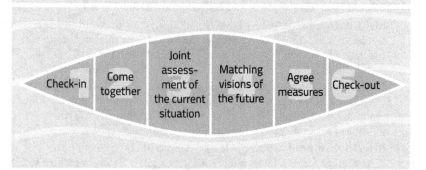

Figure 19 Axelrod's meeting canoe as the standard meeting agenda (Source: Axelrod, 2014)

The universal meeting agenda – also known as the meeting canoe (Figure 19) – by Richard Axelrod (Axelrod, 2014) functions in a very similar way. Special care is taken to engage with the participants at each meeting and to offer them a pleasant, positive environment. This standard agenda consists of six steps in total.

1. **Welcome:** How can we make a positive start possible for everyone?
2. **Introduce people and tasks:** How can we bring everyone together?
3. **Clarify the situation:** How can we create curiosity and commitment to the topic?
4. **View options and wishes:** How can we mobilise everyone's ideas?
5. **Define responsibilities:** How can we create a fair distribution of tasks?
6. **Find a coherent conclusion:** What can we learn from the meeting process?

Phil Harkins chooses another orientation metaphor for his universal agenda, namely that of the lighthouse (Harkins, 1999). His 'meeting tower' consists of four floors.

Harkins' meeting tower:

1. Status quo: What's up?

What situation are we in?

2. **Consequences:** What's so?

What does this mean for us specifically?

3. Options/solutions: What's possible?

How can we respond to that?

4. Responsibilities: Let's go!

Who will do what – and by when?

These and the other two generic agendas enable you to structure a meeting agenda and can provide gentle orientation.

↑ Following these rather strategic nudges for orientation through multiple meetings, let's move on to some short-term help for more clarity in individual meetings.

Micro Navigation: Orientation in Individual Meetings

→ You should now be familiar with the basic idea of Navicons from the previous section. In this subchapter, you will learn how to use Navicons in group discussions.

↑ In addition to **Navicons (Figure 20)**, we will also introduce other nudges for more orientation in a meeting, such as the Meet-Up Canvas as a meeting visualiser or smaller nudges such as PowerPoint Navigator, the Agenda Tracker or the Conversation Connector. In addition, we offer some hints on useful digital nudges for better orientation in virtual meetings.

→ First, however, to the use of Navicons as orientation nudges throughout the entire meeting process from preparation to appraisal.

You can use Navicons in four different ways:

1. As a planning tool or for preparing meetings.
2. As signal cards in meetings.
3. As a form of interaction at the beginning and during meetings.
4. For ex-post analysis and the improvement of meetings.

→ When *preparing* a session, you can use Navicons for your own orientation by placing the four cards in front of you in this order:

Context
Clarifying the overall situation

Details
Facts, figures, background

Looking back
Development, history, origin

Planning
Next steps, the future

Now think about how to engage with participants from the outset and orientate them about the context before briefly reviewing what progress has been made. Leave time for this overview and review before diving into any details with your colleagues. Don't forget to plan enough time at the end of the meeting to discuss the next steps, define responsibilities and possibly decide on a follow-up date.

At the *beginning* of the meeting, you can use Navicons to ensure that time is used productively during the session. After you have briefly written down and presented the proposed agenda items on a flipchart, ask everyone present to stick a small Post-it note next to the agenda item that seems most important to them. Then ask them to point an upward arrow on the piece of paper if they want a contextual discussion on the subject, a downward arrow down if they want more facts and details, or an arrow pointing left if they want to discuss what has been happening recently.

The arrow should point to the right if someone wants to plan a topic or discuss its future. Due to the placement and concentration of the yellow notes, you will know immediately what the 'hot' issues of the meeting are from the participants' perspective as well as what their information and discussion needs are.

You can do this shortly before the official start of the meeting since it acts as a nudge for everyone to be on time and have a say in the weighting of agenda items. The meeting agenda shown in the illustration is called the **Agenda Tracker (Figure 21)**. If it remains visible throughout the entire meeting and is tracked, it can act as a nudge not to deviate from the topic as well as showing each participant what is currently being discussed. You could also present the planned agenda path more imaginatively (e.g. as a racetrack) and monitor the content accordingly by deleting completed items as they are dealt with.

During the meeting, you can use the Navicons in two ways. First of all, similar to their use in the agenda, that is, as interaction and prioritisation aids (see also Boden, 1995), and secondly as signal cards for participants to

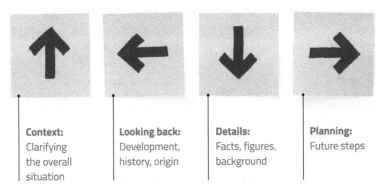

Context:
Clarifying the overall situation

Looking back:
Development, history, origin

Details:
Facts, figures, background

Planning:
Future steps

Figure 20 Navicons as a planning tool

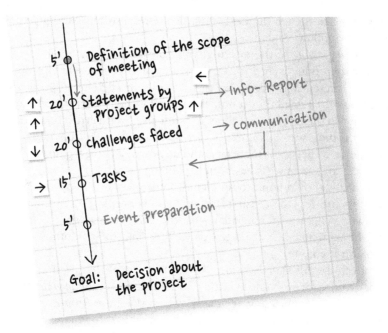

Figure 21 Navicons as a feedback tool on the agenda items in a meeting

indicate (more or less discreetly) their need for a discussion about that item. To help you, we have provided a Navicon **Bookmark** with this book for you to try out some of these ideas. Try it!

The first time you try this, you will only need small Post-it notes. For essential discussion points, these can be used, for example, to indicate the points worth pursuing further on a PowerPoint slide, poster or flipchart. In this way, a presentation which is part of a meeting can be aligned much more closely to the real interests of the listeners (Figure 22).

This type of Navicon use is also very suitable in combination with a Meet-Up Canvas, which you will get to know shortly.

The two golden rules when using Navicons in this way are:

1. First talk about the points on which the most Navicons were placed.
2. If possible, begin with the upward-pointing Navicons. Diving into details or making plans is pointless if the overall context is not yet clear to everyone.

For their second use during a meeting, you must place the Navicons on the meeting table as **Signal Cards**. You can find print templates on our

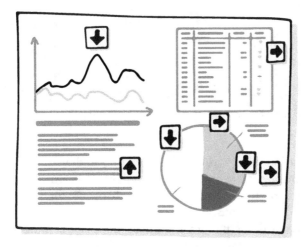

Figure 22 Navicons as a prioritisation aid during a meeting (Source: MeetingLAB, European Central Bank)

website www.meetup-book.com or as the previously mentioned bookmark. If someone feels that a discussion is not progressing productively, he or she can discreetly display a card to request a change of direction or level (e.g. from details back to an overview or from the status quo to the next steps).

This way of using Navicons also works very well in desktop and video conferencing. Without interrupting others while they are speaking, a signal can be sent that a change of discussion mode is suggested. To this end, we recommend making the four Navicon arrows standard buttons for any online meeting software you have (this can often be done by the user).

↓ In addition to the four Navicon cards, you will also find some other signal cards in the Appendix and on this book's dedicated website. These include the Dead End card (for conversations you don't think are going anywhere), the Break Time card, the Theme Park card (similar to the Parking Space in the Meet-Up Canvas) or the Joker card for particularly creative ideas (Figure 23).

Navicons can also be used as a diagnostic tool to give you useful information about the progress of a meeting. Ask the minute-taker to keep a tally sheet of the four different Navicon conversation segments. If he or she adds up the number of overview, detail, review and planning dialogues in a session, a profile of the entire meeting is

Figure 23 The future Navicon and two other signalisation cards

created. Starting with a square, a short line is drawn downwards for each detailed discussion and one to the right is drawn for each future-oriented conversation. The same thing happens for the other two Navicon arrow directions.

Evaluation of the resulting pattern will reveal the dominant modes of conversation. Was the meeting shrouded in detailed talks as in the second and third images in Figure 24 or was it more planning focused as in the first image? The Navicons allow you to visualise the respective conversation modes graphically for each session and draw insightful conclusions for future meetings. For example, did you spend less time looking back and more time planning ahead, or did you spend too much time talking in general terms rather than tackling the details? The summation of the Navicons gives you a quick, visual answer to such questions.

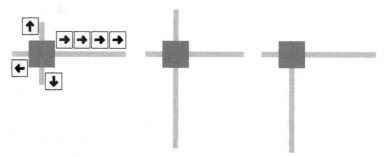

Figure 24 Different meeting profiles after adding all Navicons

→ As mentioned above, Navicons can also be used in conjunction with another orientation tool during your session – the *Meet-Up Canvas* (Figure 25). This is a particularly useful nudge for constant orientation during a meeting. The Navicons are placed in the different sections of a Meet-Up

Canvas by the participants, and this helps to ensure the issues, facts or tasks are discussed according to their priority.

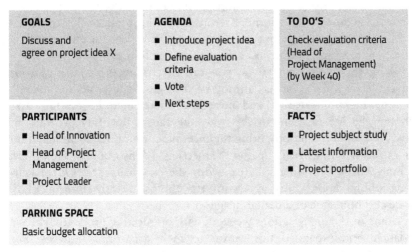

Figure 25 The Meet-Up Canvas for orientation in meetings

The **Meet-Up Canvas** itself, however, helps when preparing for the meeting to consider what is important (e.g. goals, participants, preliminary information and agenda items). As a simple Word document or poster on the wall with six zones, it is the exact opposite of a PowerPoint presentation because you stay on one page during the entire session instead of switching to a new slide every few minutes.

During the meeting, the canvas offers constant orientation and an overview. It shows what has already been discussed and what still needs to be discussed. It is a container and presentation framework for tasks, facts and decisions. By recording all useful contributions, participants feel heard and respected. It also helps you understand the people you are working with – their (technical) backgrounds and roles – through short profiles in the participant section of the canvas.

After the meeting, the completed canvas is visible proof that the meeting has taken place. It shows what has been discussed and provides immediate documentation of the tasks.

With the Meet-Up Canvas, you create a nudge so that the leader can think about the meeting goals in advance, who ought to be present and what the essential agenda items are. He or she must also consider what information needs to be obtained in advance.

The Parking Space – another section of the Meet-Up Canvas – has room for issues that arise during the meeting but are not directly related. These are written down in note form or recorded on a Post-it note. This prevents endless detailed discussions that have nothing to do with the purpose of the meeting, resulting in time lost and general irritation.

With the Meet-Up Canvas, you can determine the course of your meeting. Tick off what has already been discussed (as with the Agenda Tracker mentioned earlier) and immediately note down the resulting tasks in the 'To Do' section. In this way, the canvas not only provides an overview and orientation during the meeting but is also a documentation of the tasks to be carried out after the meeting. To distribute this to others, simply create a photograph (e.g. with the free Microsoft Office Lens smartphone app). This app converts photos directly into a PDF, a PowerPoint slide or a digital image.

Some of the organisations we work with on meeting productivity have adapted and expanded this canvas to their departmental needs. For example, we have observed how a compliance meeting canvas has improved a legal department's meetings.

To design a Meet-Up Canvas yourself and adapt it for your organisation, you need to create additional zones on the canvas for recurring topics. Examples of such zones include 'risks', 'relevant standards and laws', 'ongoing activities/projects' or 'future events'. Depending on their importance, this means a relatively large or small area on the canvas. In general, however, your session canvas should not include more than nine sections.

The *Canvas Construction Kit* provides you with a proven basic framework with place holders, which you can equip with corresponding block suggestions.

The following illustration shows the basic frame with spaces for small, medium and large blocks. Large blocks are the core aspects of the meeting such as the agenda, while small blocks represent secondary issues such as legal matters. The wide blocks depict overarching features, such as the Parking Space.

The basic framework consists of four areas:

> **Preparation:** At the top left, use these blocks to help you prepare for the meeting – participants, organisational preparations or tasks for the team.

> **Implementation:** At the centre top, use these blocks to help you during the meeting – the agenda, financial figures or essential facts.
> **Post-processing:** At the top right, use blocks to help you follow up – a to-do list or milestones before the next meeting.
> **Base:** Below, use this block a foundation stone for the entire meeting – as a Parking Space for issues that are not part of the meeting and will be filed for later discussion. You can also use the lower area as a Scrumboard and divide it into three areas: 'Tasks', 'Underway' and 'Done'.

Other possible block names might be, for example, risks, legal issues, competition, events, or industry trends. It can also be useful to reserve an empty block for suggestions during the meeting.

Try creating your own canvas that helps structure and document your meetings clearly (Figure 26).

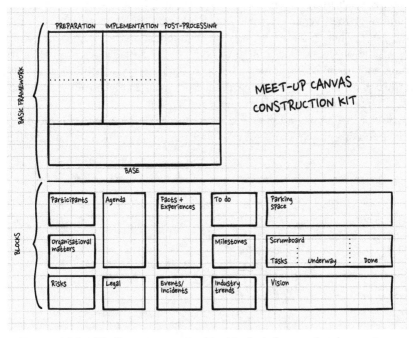

Figure 26 Meet-Up Canvas construction kit with a basic framework and suggestions for other blocks

Of course, even with a Meet-Up Canvas, it is not always possible to avoid slide presentations altogether. However, this medium is particularly problematic for orientation, since the distribution of information over many individual slides destroys the overview and orientation (in the case of alternatives such as prezi.com, this is somewhat better due to the zooming feature it incorporates). Furthermore, it is difficult to grasp an argument solely on the basis of bullet-point lists (since the individual points are not connected), especially if each slide looks virtually identical thanks to CI (corporate identity) guidelines and leaves little room for manoeuvre. It is also a real challenge to be engaged as a listener at a frontal presentation. For this particular problem, we have already recommended the periodic use of Navicons on particularly full slides.

To reduce the navigation problem during long presentations, it is also a good idea to insert a **Presentation Navigator** on the top left or lower edge of slides as shown in Figure 27.

This small nudge prompts us to understand what is visible now in the context of the overall presentation. In addition, viewers can see from the navigator when their input will be required. This need not necessarily be visible on every slide, but the navigator can be faded in from time to time, which is an excellent way of keeping your audience's attention, especially in virtual meetings. A good navigator also depicts the progress of the presentation – how much there is to go.

So that the conversation does not become too fragmented – for example, at the end of a presentation – or take place in ping-pong mode, we would like

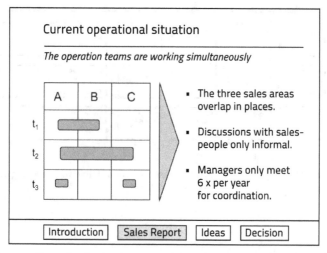

Figure 27 Example of a simple presentation navigator as an orientation nudge

to recommend another orientation nudge, the **Conversation Connector**. It sounds complicated but the principle is very straightforward.

Although the four Navicons help considerably with orientation during a conversation, sometimes it is simply not enough to signal that you want to immerse yourself in detail or to go ahead with planning. Sometimes, more specific signals are needed to maintain orientation. From our experience in complex discussions, *connectors* (connection hints) can be useful orientation nudges by making it clear how people are reacting to what has just been said. Incidentally, this is extremely helpful for online sessions in chat mode. By explicitly linking statements, everyone's orientation is maintained and there is a central theme running through the discussion.

This idea came from the famous organisational researcher Karl Weick (Weick, 1995). He calls this approach 'extracted cues', that is, explicit hints that signal what kind of contribution you are making to the conversation. We think this is one of the most effective nudges ever for avoiding confusion or frustration in business meetings. The basic rule of this behavioural nudge is that every word contribution must establish an explicit *connection to what is being said*. You should, therefore, always state your intention briefly before speaking, and this should refer directly to the last contribution (when chatting online, the point of reference is often the penultimate entry). What at first seems a bit cumbersome, quickly becomes routine and is usually the rule in North America, where they are well-versed in the service industry.

For example, instead of saying: 'I think our problem is completely different, namely Y,' according to the connector approach this sentence would have to begin: 'Mark thinks the problem is because of X. I'd like to *add* another possible focus, Y.' This formulation has little to do with diplomacy, but much to do with orientation in meetings. The signalling effect of 'adding' indicates the discussion is about to be supplemented by further options. Consider statements like, 'none of this makes any sense'. Such sweeping statements do not make for a productive conversation. Instead, argue specifically, for example, by saying, 'I agree with points A and B, but I see point C differently because . . . '.

In general, we (and some of our colleagues) differentiate and teach the following types of connection notes in conversations:

> **Confirmation:** I agree with X's point because . . .
> **Explanation:** I would like to illustrate this point with an example . . .
> **Modification:** I would like to vary this argument slightly . . .
> **Validation:** So your main concern is . . . ?
> **Evaluation:** What I find difficult about this procedure is . . .
> **Addition:** Can we continue to think through this idea by . . .

Instead of simply making your own point, try to pick up on what has been said by others and deliberately associate your contribution with theirs. This not only clarifies the nature of *your input* and the *direction* of the conversation, but it also shows that you are listening to your colleagues and respecting their opinions. You will notice after a short while that this comes almost intuitively.

← We have now discussed some *verbal* and *visual* orientation nudges and illustrated them with examples. To do this, we have mainly used signalisation, pre-structuring and feedback nudges.

↑ Now it's time to provide some orientation in this chapter by deciding which of the nudges are most relevant to you personally. Select what you can use immediately, what you want to try out and what you might want to come back to later.

Orientation Nudges at a Glance

	Nudge	Nudging principle	Yes, from now on	I'll try it out	Maybe later
Macro-orientation	Meeting Landscape	Feedback and mistake anti-cipation	○	○	○
	Meeting Typology	Pre-structuring and signalling	○	○	○
	Visible Clock	Signalling	○	○	○
	Timer	Signalling	○	○	○
	Stand Up (No chairs)	Pre-structuring	○	○	○
Micro-orientation	Navicons	Signalling	○	○	○
	Signal Cards	Signalling	○	○	○
	Agenda Tracker	Feedback and signalling	○	○	○
	Bookmark	Signalling	○	○	○
	Meet-Up Canvas	Pre-structuring and feedback	○	○	○
	PowerPoint Navigator	Signalling	○	○	○
	Conversation Connector	Signalling	○	○	○

CHAPTER 7

Involvement
Nudges for Better Involvement

← He wanted a proper exchange rather than an endless PowerPoint presentation, some real engagement with the content – and he got it. We are talking about the Chairman of a Frankfurt-based bank, who came up with a new way to entice members of the Executive Board to get more involved in their regular meetings.

He had the six most important slides from his presentation printed out in large format and placed them in the meeting room. Up until then, all eight executive board members would sit in comfortable armchairs and passively watch one slide after another – and he wanted to change this. His goal was to activate himself and his colleagues not only physically, but also mentally because all too often, any discussion was superficial at best. As the board members rose from their armchairs and began to walk from one large-format slide to another, something amazing happened. Without a projected slide on the wall and the hum of the beamer, an atmosphere of calm concentration began to fill the room. People really started to get to grips with the details and there was a buzz of animated conversation. One person even took a pen and drew a circle between two existing decision options with a question mark saying, 'and there could be a third option'. At this point, someone else interjected: 'By a third option, do you mean a combination of options 1 and 2 or something completely new?' Interestingly the content hadn't changed from the usual set of slides for such a meeting. It was the change in infrastructure and the associated physical activity and proximity to the slides that enabled a completely different set of conversations at eye-level and prompted more in-depth discussions in terms of content (see Figure 28).

This **Gallery Walk** nudge will show you how you can already trigger a more productive atmosphere by changing the infrastructure, and you don't need to be the CEO of a large bank. All you require is a little extra space in the meeting room and the possibility to print slides in a large format – for small groups of up to four people, A3 format is sufficient.

Figure 28 Gallery walk as a stand-up meeting format

 In this chapter, you will learn about other *infrastructure nudges* that you can use to encourage people in meetings to be more directly involved. If you don't want to be too subtle in your approach, you can use *procedure and rule* nudges and, depending on the situation, you can choose nudges that directly or indirectly prompt greater involvement.

You will see there are a variety of nudges to help you support involvement during meetings. You will also find nudges to encourage involvement *before* and *after* the meeting. For example, you could use a (voluntary!) creativity nudge in meetings after 5 p.m. by allowing participants a small amount of alcohol, which has been proven to stimulate creativity. With the nudges in this chapter, you can discover the hidden talents of your quieter colleagues and how much you can achieve in a short time.

Direct Involvement through Procedures and Rules

A direct and handy procedure nudge to entice quieter people to participate through the principle of pre-structuring is the **Think-Pair-Share** nudge, which structures involvement in three stages (see Figure 29).

First, ask participants to write down their ideas alone (think). Then give them time to exchange their thoughts with one other person (pair) before each team shares its ideas with the whole group (share) (Azlina, 2010).

Figure 29 The think-pair-share approach to involvement in meetings

If you allow each participant to write down their own ideas first without being influenced by others, this leads to a higher number of more original ideas (Van Gundy, 1984). This approach is also known as the *nominal group principle* and contrasts with traditional brainstorming, in which ideas are (erroneously) classified into groups (Dennis & Valacich, 1994). If you allow participants to exchange their ideas in pairs before they are discussed in plenary, you will help them develop fresher ideas and gain greater acceptance of them by the whole group. It has been scientifically shown that when participants exchange ideas in pairs, they receive the social validation that helps them generate more 'outside the box' ideas than if they discussed them directly with the whole meeting.

At the same time, it has been shown that ideas that have been pre-discussed and tested in small groups find more acceptance in the plenum.

As a variant, in a meeting with two people, you can limit yourself just to think-pair so that both participants first generate ideas for themselves and then exchange them. However, they can also focus on pair-share, especially where large groups are concerned.

Try to visualise how you can split a large group into smaller groups for the first part. The pair-share option is also worth employing if the energy level in the room is low because it can be more stimulating to work in pairs. If the total number of participants is odd, you can, of course, form a group of three.

Whatever option you choose, Think-Pair-Share (or a greater focus on think-pair or pair-share), the whole process doesn't have to take long. For example, with the help of the **Time Boxing** nudge in think-pair-share, you can give each individual five minutes to generate ideas, then ten minutes to exchange ideas in twos. Depending on the size of the group, you can then give between 20 minutes (for four people) and 40 minutes (for eight people). With the Time Boxing nudge, you temporarily create a new default value for each stage. By applying the **Boss Goes Last** nudge, make sure that the team with the most senior (in terms of organisational hierarchy) person in the room presents its ideas last so that others do not try to curry favour by copying the boss.

Concerning time management, it helps a lot if you specify a **Maximum Number** of ideas that can be presented. When teams have to agree on their best two or three ideas, presentations become more efficient. For inactive or reluctant participants, you can specify a **Minimum Number** of solutions or ideas.

If you then want to decide as a meeting which are the best ideas, you can use the **Dotmocracy** nudge to award small sticky dots that participants can use to rate each other's contributions (Public Health Ontario, 2010). In this evaluation nudge, make sure that you give participants dots in at least two different colours, telling them that one colour (e.g. yellow) should be used for particularly original ideas and another colour (e.g. blue) for ideas that are quick and easy to implement. Without this distinction between originality and feasibility, participants tend to limit themselves to approving ideas that can be realised more easily (Rietzschel, Nijstad & Stroebe, 2010). In addition, have the participants write down in advance which ideas they want to vote for so they are not influenced by the votes of the other participants.

If peer pressure is likely to be a problem, have a 'secret ballot' with the chairperson sticking up all the dots at the same time. A break during the meeting is suitable for this purpose so that everyone can look at the overall results together. By making participant feedback visible, you are also making it available for future use. We recommend that you include the voting results in the meeting documentation by taking a digital photo. This will simplify access later.

↑ In previous sections, you have already seen how different nudges can be cleverly combined to encourage people to participate more. You can use the Think-Pair-Share and Time Boxing nudges to ensure the time spent is productive, creative and fair. In the following sections, you will find more nudges, both to make participants' voices heard and for greater involvement *before* a meeting. Various creativity nudges, such as the ABSURD nudge, will demonstrate how you can have fun getting more people involved.

In addition to the Dotmocracy nudge, there is another way to make the votes of participants visible with the help of some rules. You can choose between three different feedback rules – one is simple and the others are more complex. Use the simple **Plus-Delta** nudge (Figure 30) to share the positive aspects (Plus) as well as things that are not yet ideal (Delta).

If this two-way split is not sufficient, you can use the **Feedback Matrix** nudge that is often used in design-thinking meetings (see Figure 31). Here, participants can note down and share their priorities, wishes, questions and ideas. Priorities are located in the upper-left section and are marked +.

Write down anything to which you could say, 'I like this ... '. The upper-right section is for direct or implied wishes – marked with a triangle – in which you can write down anything you would change. The lower-left section is for questions arising and the bottom-right section is for improvement ideas (marked with a light bulb). This nudge is particularly useful when discussing open wishes and questions.

For idea improvement, you can use the **Hollywood** nudge with the PPCO formula in your meetings (Figure 32). This is how the Hollywood writers of

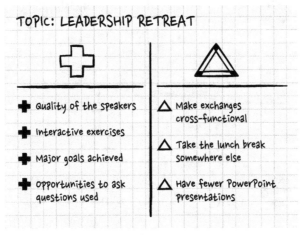

Figure 30 Plus-Delta nudge

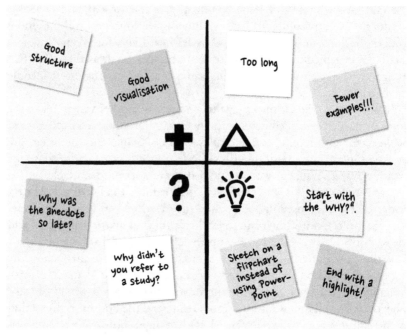

Figure 31 Feedback matrix nudge

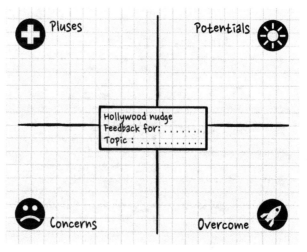

Figure 32 Hollywood nudge

TV series such as House M.D. give themselves feedback. With this nudge, the entire group can share the **P**luses and **P**otentials (in cases where there is room for improvement). The second part of the nudge is the challenge to generate productive feedback. Each participant may express their **C**oncerns (e.g. about a presentation); however, for each concern they raise, participants must demonstrate a coping strategy to **O**vercome the problem.

We have often used the Hollywood nudge in meetings and workshops and it really does lead to positive and productive feedback.

It is best to combine this and the other two feedback nudges with the Time Boxing nudge, for example, by allowing a maximum of five minutes per person for feedback. With the Hollywood nudge, you can use the first minute for the plus points. Allow participants to list the potentials only in the remaining four minutes and emphasise that a concern may only be expressed if at least one suggestion for overcoming it can be offered. In this way, everyone learns how to give regulated feedback in a productive way.

→ Templates for the various feedback nudges can be found on the website for this book at www.meetup-book.com.

While you will use the nudges presented so far mostly during meetings, the following **Check Prior Knowledge** nudge gives you the chance to involve the participants *before* the meeting. With this nudge, you can skilfully familiarise participants with the subject matter through the invitation. Ask everyone coming to write a relevant sentence on the topic, which you then put alongside that person's name on the list of attendees (Figure 33).

For example, if you want to discuss the use of strategy work tools in a meeting, you can ask each participant to write a statement in advance about their use of strategy work tools. This striking sentence would then give everyone an impression, in the run-up to the meeting, of what issues were of concern to others. You could also use these statements during the session and ask participants to explain or comment on their statement in greater detail. A variant of this nudge would be if you, as leader, asked each participant in advance to share his or her exclusive knowledge with you by e-mail or in person. This is especially helpful because sharing exclusive knowledge seldom takes place in the meeting context (the common knowledge effect), as discussed at the beginning of this book.

If you want to ensure a positive attitude at the beginning of a meeting, begin in the same way as a well-known Swiss company with a 'success round'. Before getting down to business, everyone shares a success from the past week. In the company concerned, this resulted in a change of attitude towards meetings from the negative discussion of problems to positive success stories. With this **Success Round** nudge, employees are also

MEETING PARTICIPANTS

Name	Comment
Clive Davenport	"SWOT analysis is still the best."
Dr. Mike Wilson	"We should try some agile methods."
Dr. Richard Darnill	"Not another SWOT analysis, please!"
Susannah Goodson	"We should introduce an empathy card."
Neil Corlett	"Fewer PowerPoints – more "hands-on" with flipcharts."

Figure 33 List of participants and their individual comments on a topic

sensitised during the week to remember their successes so they can share them at the next meeting.

Another nudge for getting people involved before or at the very beginning of a meeting is the **Mindful Moment** nudge, which Google uses to help its employees become more creative. According to their Chief Innovation Evangelist, Frederik Pferdt, the 'mindful moment' is a completely normal impulse before creative sessions by focusing people's attention on themselves, their colleagues and on the meeting itself through a brief (e.g. five-minute) meditation. It has been proven that this nudge leads to more ideas as well as more original ideas. We took part in just such a meditation and were amazed at the strong effect it had regarding the perception and presence of ourselves and other participants.

↓ The Dutch researcher Lorenza Colzato and her team were able to show in a study that two types of meditation lead to improved creativity. The first uses the principle of 'open observation', in which non-reactive, friendly observation is practised from moment to moment as experiences emerge. This form of meditation has led to the improvement of idea generation, i.e. to the support of divergent thinking. The second form of meditation uses the principle of 'focused attention', in which focusing and observing an object or activity is practised, such as noticing one's own breath. This has led to improvements in the evaluation and selection of ideas, thereby supporting convergent thinking (Colzato, Szapora, Lippelt & Hommel, 2017).

You can integrate both 'open observation' and 'focused attention' in a five-minute meditation before the meeting or at the very beginning to aid both the divergent (creative) and convergent thinking processes of your participants.

Another nudge to encourage greater creativity is the **Begin Sentence** nudge. Have you experienced a situation in meetings when people don't join in because they think they are not creative enough or that their ideas are either too boring or too outrageous? You can counteract this effect by relieving participants of the pressure to be creative themselves by starting with predefined sentences. An easy way to dispel any doubts is to suggest sentences that begin, 'I'm only thinking out loud ... '. This signals to others that the following idea may be completely crazy so please consider it as such and don't criticise it immediately. You can either implicitly introduce this nudge as a participant yourself by simply saying, 'I'm just thinking out loud here but ... ' at the beginning of a sentence or explicitly asking everyone to 'think out loud' for the next five minutes. You can also introduce other sentence beginnings to stimulate creativity. For example, if you want your participants to advance the ideas of others, introduce the following rule. Instead of 'yes, but ... ', the ideas of others may only be commented on with 'yes, and ... '. This technique is used in design-thinking meetings to develop ideas by using a positive connotation.

If participants prefer a more diplomatic approach, then adopt the role of devil's advocate with the opening phrase, 'If I were playing devil's advocate here, then ... '. Make this a general rule for the entire meeting time or for individual sections, perhaps, ten minutes before the break, during which 'thinking out loud' is allowed.

Sentence Function

'I'm just thinking out loud ... '

Articulating unfinished thoughts, no criticism
'Yes, and ... ' instead of 'yes, but ... '
Building on the ideas of others
'If I were playing devil's advocate here, then ... '
Expressing criticism without attacking

An unconventional variation of this nudge is the **Meeting Zones** nudge, where you can use adhesive tape to create zones in the meeting room that have a similar effect. With the help of simple adhesive tape, for example, you can quickly mark out the 'thinking out loud' zone'(Figure 34).

In addition to the 'thinking out loud' zone, a 'yes, and . . . ' zone and a 'devil's advocate' zone can also be set up. You will see that it can be really fun to get involved with the respective signals within these zones.

← On the subject of zones, former Swiss national ice-hockey coach, Kent Ruhnke, drew a line with the help of adhesive tape and created two zones in the team changing room. He asked his players to stand on one side of the line if they felt they were winning the game through technique and to stand on the other side of the line if they felt they were winning through physical effort. After all the players had decided, interestingly, there were more players on the technique side than on the physical side. At this point, Kent Ruhnke stood up, went over to the line and said: 'We can only win when we combine technique and physical effort.' This image remained in the minds of his players and, from then on, Kent Ruhnke only had to pick up a roll of tape for everyone to know what he was thinking.

If you – like Kent Ruhnke – want to leave a lasting impression on the people in your meetings, then following the **ABSURD** nudge is the ideal solution (Figure 35). With it, you can playfully ensure more creativity and

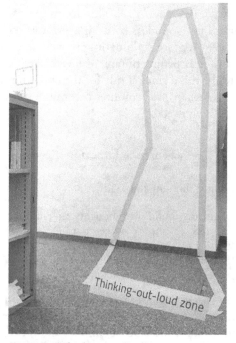

Figure 34 'Thinking out loud' zone in meetings
(Source: MCM Institute)

Figure 35 The six elements of the ABSURD nudge

involvement when solving problems. Involvement can, may and must be fun at times, especially when it comes to solving complex issues and finding creative solutions. Laughter promotes a positive atmosphere, reduces hierarchy barriers and has a positive effect on solution-finding (Kangasharju & Nikko, 2009). Use this fun factor nudge – pick out one of the following suggestions and motivate your meeting to some positive involvement:

Anti: How can we make this problem worse? (Flip-flop technique)

Big Spender: How would we solve the problem if money didn't matter? (Croesus technique)

Superhuman: How would Lara Croft/the Dalai Lama/Google solve the problem? (Superhuman technique)

Uncool: How would the problem have been solved thirty years ago? (Nostalgia technique)

ROFL (Rolling on the floor laughing): Which solution would you least expect from us? (Self-irony technique)

Dream: What would you choose if you had one wish? (Aladdin technique)

With these ABSURD questions, you can encourage some humorous, self-ironic, exaggerated and, therefore, productive behaviour. With the flip-flop technique, try to make the problem worse first instead of solving it directly. You can then formulate solutions from the worsening sugges-tions. Instead of thinking immediately about how to retain existing cus-tomers, think about what you would need to do to lose every customer as quickly as possible. Based on these destructive ideas, you should then think about how you can convert them so that the customers remain with you. This technique demonstrably leads to better ideas than if you are looking directly for solutions (Eppler, Hoffmann & Pfister, 2014). You'll also see that it can be great fun being destructive. With the Croesus technique, money and budgets play no role in the first step – just develop ideas without financial restrictions. Now, consider how you might implement the ideas from the first step within the existing budget restrictions. For the superhuman technique, imagine how your superheroes, such as Lara Croft, the Dalai Lama or even companies like Google, would approach and solve the problem. What perspective does the superhero have? Allow yourself to use the supernatural abilities of your superhero in the first step to create some seemingly unrealistic ideas for yourself. Only then can you consider which aspects of this solution could be used to solve problems in your existing situation. With the nostalgia technique, you imagine how the problem would have been solved – say – thirty years ago. Compare this nostalgic problem solving with your current problem-solving strategy. If there is no difference, then think about how you can solve the problem using the modern technology available today. With the self-irony tech-nique, you can invite the participants to question their own approach and consciously 'poke fun'. These ideas will probably be so absurd that every-one will be in fits of laughter by the end. That is why we have chosen the popular online initialism ROFL for this technique, which stands for 'rolling on the floor laughing'. New ways to solve problems can arise from solutions that you would not expect from your own organisation or team. The Aladdin technique, whereby all wishes are granted, helps reveal unconscious assumptions or obstacles and offers ways to circumvent them.

For example, if your wish is for the entire team to all meet in the same room, then the spatial distance between you is probably making collabor-ation difficult. Building on this, you will consider how virtual meetings could be optimised in the future so that the geographical separation is no longer so critical. Incidentally, you will find some helpful suggestions for virtual meetings in the final chapter of this book.

So you can see how people are encouraged to participate through a simple question and that it might be fun. Feel free to tell us about your experiences with ABSURD questions via the website linked to this book.

↑ The procedures and rules presented here help you in a straightforward way to inspire participants and motivate them to productive involvement. But when it comes to helping people to be more productive in a subtle way, you can do so with infrastructure and artefact nudges. This is exactly what the next section is all about.

Indirect Involvement through Infrastructure and Artefacts

In the introductory example, we demonstrated how a familiar meeting room can be used differently by printing the slides in a large format to encourage productive involvement. In the following sections, you will find further nudges on how to modify existing rooms and how to design new rooms and artefacts.

← Have you noticed how often meeting rooms are designed so that everyone sits at tables and everything is organised so that people stare at projections on the screen? Or as a consultant from Interbrand – one of the world's largest strategy consultancies – put it: 'People prefer to look at slides on the wall instead of looking at their brains.' In this section, we will encourage you to think consciously about changing the space, environment and artefacts in your meetings so your participants become more engaged and involved. After all, we know that our environment affects our behaviour (Doorley & Witthoft, 2011).

It may be an unusual location that stimulates participants to participate and come up with new ideas because of different surroundings. For example, some start-ups go to an Alpine co-working facility for a week to be inspired by nature and the tranquillity of the mountains. However, you don't have to change rooms immediately or travel – you can also 'hack' ordinary meeting rooms.

One way to enhance a meeting room is to use the Gallery Walk, as described earlier, by printing slides in a large format. You can then augment these with the help of the **Einstein** nudge. Einstein recorded his thoughts each day with pen and paper and often found that his sketches provided him with new insights, which he confirmed with the statement, 'my pen is smarter than I am'. This knowledge gain is also known as the 'free ride effect' (Shimojima, 1999). Be an Einstein and go one step further by leaving an ample white border around the slides when printing the posters (see Figure 36). Give everyone a pen so they can comment on the slide content and physically add ideas from the discussion to the printout. We have seen for ourselves that managers can achieve higher productivity and make better decisions with the help of a simple pen and paper (Eppler & Pfister, 2010).

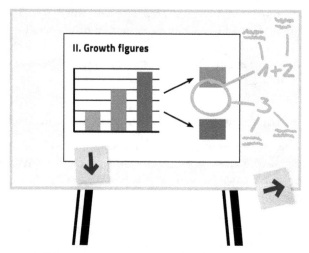

Figure 36 Slides with pen annotations and sticky notes (Einstein-nudge)

An often-overlooked detail regarding the **Pens** nudge is to make sure that participants have a pen and that this pen works. Only then can everyone contribute on an equal footing and can multiple ideas be written down simultaneously. We have observed how, in many meetings at a strategic brand consultancy, the presence of only one pen among the entire group inhibits involvement.

↓ At Google, the facility management team is responsible for ensuring that there are enough functioning pens and Post-it notes available every week so that the teams can visually support their discussions on whiteboards. Another interesting fact is that the maximum distance of any employee at Google from a coffee bar is frequently quoted as 10 metres, but the distance from whiteboards and functioning pens is often much less.

If you have annotated your discussion with working pens and then want to record them for your colleagues who were unable to attend the meeting, then the **Gallery Video** nudge is a great choice. Make a short smartphone video (no longer than three minutes) in which the leader or another designated person walks and talks through the slides and summarises what was said and commented on. This video is also a nudge to document the meeting and simplifies the follow-up stages considerably.

As well as large-format slides, a change in the table layout can ensure that the participants are encouraged to participate more. In this **Spatial Design** nudge, for example, arrange the tables for groups of two or four, which promotes more direct exchanges.

Figure 37 A sticky note table for portable visualisation
(Source: SoapStudio)

In meetings and workshops with executives at Hilti, among others, we made the concept of pairwork the main feature and always put two desks together. In addition, each pair has its own flipchart and pinboard to discussions visually. This **Visual Documentation** nudge enabled intensive exchanges to take place throughout the day and some pairs even starting referring to this set-up as their 'island'. As an alternative to the flipchart and pinboard, you could also use portable foam boards, which can be turned into a whiteboard with the help of a whiteboard cover. You can now also buy desks which are effectively giant notepads (see Figure 37). This **Portable Visualisation** nudge not only helps to visualise agenda items during the meeting but also allows them to be removed from the meeting room to be worked on further.

The portable whiteboard, pen annotation and the use of (colour-coded) Post-it notes are all examples of how making involvement visible is an excellent way to encourage more involvement in your meetings (Schulz-Hardt & Brodbeck, 2012). This nudge connects people and highlights the different voices, recording them for later use in the meeting or afterwards.

↑ In the following sections, you will find simple and effective ways to visualise involvement by using digital surveys. You will also see how nudges for PowerPoint can help everyone get more involved.

With the **Visual Echo** nudge, you can create virtual surveys before, during or after the meeting by sending questions to participants via the 'Mentimeter'. For example, if you want to discuss your meeting culture or tools for strategy work, you could post questions such as: 'What adjectives would you use to describe a typical meeting in our organisation?' or 'Which tools do you use for your strategy work?' Your survey has a code that you give to participants beforehand or during the meeting. People then register on www.menti.com to take part in the survey. This website is so user-friendly that everyone can complete the questionnaire on their smart-phones during the meeting.

The survey results are then displayed to the whole group. This nudge is particularly useful at the beginning of the meeting to make participants more active and visible – or when several choices have been offered. You can then use the results as a basis for further discussion during the meeting. Due to its anonymity, even sensitive issues can be tackled with the help of this nudge. We use this nudge regularly in meetings, and it has been shown that one or two well-placed questions can be very constructive.

↓ Concerning your choice of visualisation options, Mentimeter uses the 'word cloud' format to portray the frequency of responses given. In this way, you can literally present participants with their answers and frequen-cies, which can prove surprising. Figure 38 shows that meetings in this instance are primarily perceived as 'long'. As a leader, you would now have

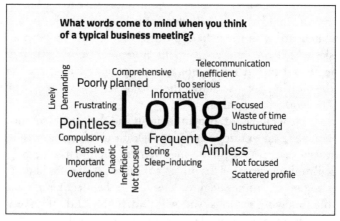

Figure 38 Word cloud for the visual representation of participant surveys
(Source: authors' own image using mentimeter.com)

the opportunity to ask those present to supplement their feedback with specific examples or anecdotes.

Following this, strategies for making meetings shorter could then be explored.

In addition to the word cloud, a matrix can be used to visualise the results of the survey. This highlights the heterogeneity of the responses, leading to a differentiated discussion.

For example, if you asked participants about their use of tools in strategy work, you can see in Figure 39 that the SWOT analysis is generally very well known, but you can also see that the answers given are very different. Some participants have never heard of the SWOT analysis, while others are familiar with it and use it frequently. This differentiated approach helps everyone gain new insights; good discussion takes place on this basis.

Graphic

The Visual Echo nudge quickly and easily gets people in meetings involved. When you use Mentimeter to ask questions at the start of a session and visually present the answers, you are implicitly telling participants that they are being taken seriously. This creates a sound foundation for further involvement during the meeting.

Another way to involve participants in a session by making your contribution visible is – believe it or not – PowerPoint. Of course, we are used to

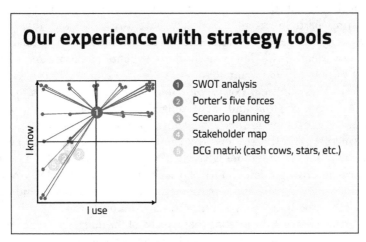

Figure 39 Matrix for the visual representation of answers
(Source: author's own image using mentimeter.com)

PowerPoint being frequently used to display (endless) sets of slides (Kernbach, Bresciani & Eppler, 2015). But how about changing the game and using PowerPoint to record content instead of playing content? For example, did you know that you can switch to editor mode in PowerPoint during a presentation (and it's only visible to you)?

With the **PowerPoint Editor** nudge, you can switch from presentation mode to edit mode to note down input and then make it visible to everyone. Prepare an empty slide – this signals that it needs to be filled – and include participant input. You can then easily use these slides during or after the meeting. Using this little PowerPoint hack, you escape from a typical presentation style and encourage your audience to be more personally involved. You can find detailed instructions for this nudge on our website.

Graphic

Another PowerPoint hack to promote involvement and focus attention on whoever is speaking is to press 'B' on your keyboard. This deactivates the projection of the slide and prevents the so-called 'split attention effect', whereby participants have to divide their attention between the speaker and the slides (Mayer & Moreno, 1998). You will be amazed at the effect the **PowerPoint Press B** nudge has on attention levels.

If you want people to remain focused at the end of a PowerPoint presentation, use the **PowerPoint Thumbnails** nudge (see Figure 40). By displaying all the slides as small images (thumbnails), you are reminding participants of what they have just seen and this is far more likely to generate comments than the timeless formula, 'are there any questions?' This can lead to a genuine discussion of the points raised – if you want it to.

↑ After these unusual PowerPoint nudges, portable whiteboards and virtual surveys, you will find more nudges in the remaining part of this chapter to encourage greater involvement through adjustments to the infrastructure. You will see how you can engage large numbers of people and why some organisations give their meetings bold labels in which openness and flying microphones play a significant role. Finally, you will encounter some unusual meeting rooms as nudges in themselves and learn why it can sometimes be a good idea to walk out of them.

Speaking of leaving the meeting room, many of the nudges presented so far work well when everyone is in one place, but what if you want to bring together a larger group or a whole crowd? Using a **Crowd Mobilisation**

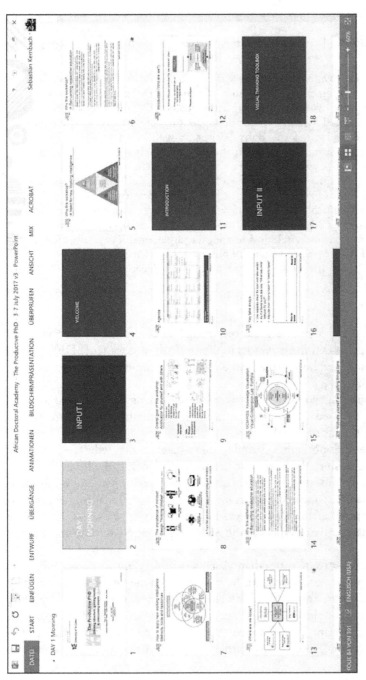

Figure 40 PowerPoint thumbnail nudge
(Source: MCM Institute)

↓ Box 6 – Learning from Other Contexts: The Hollywood Meeting Rules

What can we learn from the writers of American TV shows about productive meetings? A number of things. After all, they have had many years of experience in getting groups of creative egocentrics to write successful scripts under time pressure yet with few hard-and-fast rules. Rule No.1 is the **Baby Writer** nudge. This states that the youngest authors in the team should offer their opinions and ideas first – to give space for fresh perspectives and new impulses. There is also the **Stupid Stick** nudge – a kind of joker card or harlequin stick, which increases the fun factor. The holder may say something heretical, unrealistic or daring without having to face negative criticism. Another peculiarity of the writer's room is the **Fishbowl** nudge, with one circle inside another larger one. The inner ring is used for discussion, while the outer ring is used solely for observation, listening and offering periodic feedback.

---

nudge, we will show how the biggest online conference in Germany, re: publica, persuaded many visitors to the German broadcaster (ZDF) stand to participate – and how a collective picture of the future of television emerged from this.

In Figure 41, you can see how the designers of the ZDF stand at the congress inspired visitors to contribute to the highly visible Sankey diagram on the future of television.

The result is not only a sizeable Sankey diagram that reflects enthusiastic involvement since the image also became a work of art which was shared on social media. So, the next time you want to visualise something, think of the iconic image created here. It forms a strong emotional connection and is visible proof of a task completed together. Maybe you will want to share your collaborative efforts with the whole organisation at some point in the future?

If you want to do more than visualise people's contributions and go as far as hearing what participants have to say, then the **Open Mic** nudge may be your answer. Some organisations schedule meetings with an appealing title to make it clear that everyone can have their say. At *The Economist*, there is a meeting every Monday morning called 'The Editorial Scrum', when every staff member, regardless of status or seniority, is invited to

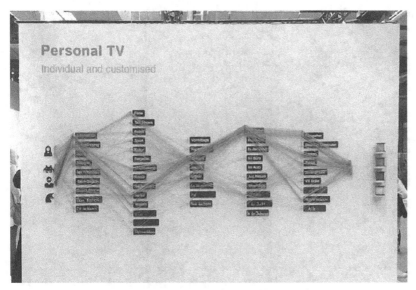

Figure 41 Sankey diagram created by conference visitor input
(Source: ZDF/republica)

present his or her ideas for stories. Only the strength and quality of the argument matters.

At large meetings or conferences, such as the d.confestival at the Hasso Plattner Institute in Potsdam, soft cube microphones are making crowd involvement far easier. This **Throwable Mic** nudge involves a Catchbox being passed on or thrown and it can be great fun (see Figure 42). At getcatchbox.com you will find the first microphone in the world designed specifically for this purpose.

At the IDEO design studio, there is a meeting called 'bits & bites' every Monday lunchtime, at which an open microphone is available. Here, any employee can share in five minutes why he or she is excited about a new digital idea. IDEO knows that a bold name for a meeting can attract the attention, curiosity and expectations of those attending. This **Bold Label** nudge has also influenced the way employees talk, while the best ideas from 'bits & bites' can be found online at **https://goo.gl/SsoizW**.

↑ At the beginning of the chapter, we talked about adapting existing spaces and have shown you many ways to modify meeting rooms so that participants can be more productive. Let's now look at

Figure 42 Throwable microphone
(Source: Catchbox)

ways to redesign whole rooms for specific purposes and how to use the world around us creatively too.

Some companies now have special meeting rooms for very specific purposes. The online agency Format D, for example, has a space like a miniature amphitheatre mainly consisting of giant steps, which means that everyone has a different visual perspective (Figure 43).

Management consultant PwC uses the latest on-screen technology to make sharing content via smartphones or tablets flexible and straightforward for all participants – eliminating the need for cumbersome projectors.

This increases people's willingness to exchange information. In contrast to digital high-tech, Google in Zurich relies on a non-digital room in which there is neither a projector nor sockets, so no one is distracted by electronics. Instead, there are writeable walls and tables with paper covers or huge Post-it notes that can be taken away after the meeting. As you can see, the **Spatial Miracle** nudge can give an entire room a unique function and encourage participants in your meetings to be more productive.

Figure 43 Amphitheatre-style arena as a nudge for different perspectives
(Source: Format D)

Our last infrastructure nudge concerns the world beyond conventional meeting rooms or offices and brings physical activity into the equation along with a change of scene. The **Nordic Talking** nudge is particularly helpful for conversations in small groups of two or three people.

↓ The so-called innovation walk – successfully practised by start-ups in Silicon Valley (Oppezzo &Schwartz, 2014) – was also already used by Kant and Kierkegaard to encourage creative thinking and mutual involvement. The expression 'walking meeting' may already be familiar, possibly from the TV series 'The West Wing', in which the President, after making a speech and heading for his limousine, holds short walking and talking meetings with his staff. In England, 'walking meetings' are now prescribed by health authorities to counteract the damage of constant sitting, the great importance of which has been made clear by statements such as 'sitting is the new smoking' (National Health Service, 2017).

Choose a flat route that is not physically demanding, take pens and paper with you and give participants between ten and thirty minutes to exchange ideas on a given topic. Make sure that there are no more than three people in a group – this is also recommended by managers at Oracle. In our experience, however, pairs work best. You can use this innovation walk, which we have renamed 'Nordic Talking', for phases in meetings when energy levels are generally rather low, such as after lunch when people may be feeling particularly drowsy. Our experience of meetings and workshops shows that participants appreciate this activity very much and they not only exchange ideas more freely but also much more openly and honestly, returning to the meeting room revitalised. At all-day meetings, Nordic Talking often means there is no need for an extra break in the middle of the afternoon. Why not try it out for yourself with a colleague? After lunch, go outside for a twenty-minute Nordic talk in the open air.

We generally recommend, whenever possible, that you first try a nudge yourself or with a small group. You may discover aspects you want to change, and you will have the added benefits of introducing a nudge based on your own experience.

→ We hope this chapter has inspired you to attempt one or two nudges to promote greater productivity in future business meetings. You can use direct approaches such as Procedures and Rules and Think-Pair-Share or ABSURD questions – or less direct ways with infrastructure or artefacts, such as the Spatial Design or Nordic Talking nudges.

These discourage unnecessary monologues, the unwelcome dominance of some individuals and turn pseudo-involvement into genuine exchanges. As you can see from the examples, a cleverly applied nudge doesn't have to cost a lot of time. It leads not only to a higher number of more original ideas, but it can be enjoyable and motivating as well.

→ Pay attention to the immediacy of involvement through these nudges and don't become too distracted by (digital) tools or gadgets. Focus on writing down ideas on Post-it notes quickly instead of spending ages installing the latest computer software. You are the 'involvement guru' who understands the tools and techniques while recognising the importance of the process and its healthy limitations. In this way, you will achieve productive involvement that is fun and produces concrete results. Don't wait too long – have the courage to try one of these nudges in your team, in pairs or even in a non-work context. You will be amazed at how much you can achieve in a short time.

Involvement Nudges at a Glance

↓ **Box 7 – Nudges for a Positive Conflict Culture**

Conflicts in meetings can really rob time and energy from everyone involved. The following nudges show you how to deal with disputes in meetings in an intelligent way. These nudges will help you to prevent conflict situations (a) from arising in the first place and (b) from 'dragging yourself and others down' in the heat of the moment.

(A)   PREVENTING CONFLICT

Have the meeting participants do a short self-assessment at the beginning of the conversation, for example, by using the notepad to sketch a smiley to indicate their current mood, thereby helping them to become more aware of their own state of mind. Alternatively, you could ask everyone present to describe their current emotional state during a short 'check-in'. This is done, for example, by airline crews at the beginning of every shift to avoid team conflicts during the flight. If you have not been able to prevent a conflict from arising, the following nudges will help you to deal with it in a productive way.

(B)   IN THE HEAT OF THE MOMENT

During tense moments, try to turn your gaze away from the conflict situation and consciously look out the window, counting quietly from one to three along the lines of 'out of sight, out of mind'. Findings from neuroscience research show that a change in body position influences our emotional mood. If you are in a conflict, your new body position – e.g. looking out the window rather than sitting at the table – will override the emotions of the conflict and help bring you about the change (Havas, Glenberg, Gutowski, Lucarelli & Davidson, 2010). Counting slowly is also a traditional trick for distracting the mind and focusing on a specific task (Valentine & Sweet, 1999).

Another way of redirecting attention in conflict situations from your head to your physical surroundings is known as 'grounding'. This technique involves consciously focusing on a tangible object nearby, such as the light fitting in the room, a pen on the table or a picture on the wall.

You can extend this approach by carrying a 'grounding object' with you, which you can look at and touch in conflict situations while keeping a particular image in mind. A well-known CEO in Switzerland has his own ritual for conflict situations; he pretends to look for something in his briefcase, but in so doing finds a small stuffed animal belonging to his daughter, which he touches briefly to calm himself down in a matter of seconds. Invent a ritual for yourself that you can rely on in crisis moments.

A third, diagnostic tactic is to evaluate your state of mind in an unbiased way by estimating your anger level in conflict situations on a scale of one to five. This process of self-evaluation quickly brings the mind back from a highly emotional state to a more analytical state. A small snack can also reduce tension (Steiner, 2011). Think, for example, of the well-known Snicker's commercial with the slogan: 'You're not you when you're hungry'.

	Nudge	Nudging principle	Yes, from now on	I'll try it out	Maybe later
Procedures and rules	Think-Pair-Share	Pre-structuring	O	O	O
	Time Boxing	Default value	O	O	O
	Boss Goes Last	Pre-structuring	O	O	O
	Maximum Number	Default value	O	O	O
	Minimum Number	Default value	O	O	O
	Dotmocracy	Pre-structuring	O	O	O
	Plus-Delta	Visible feedback	O	O	O
	Feedback Matrix	Visible feedback	O	O	O
	Hollywood	Visible feedback	O	O	O
	Check Prior Knowledge	Default value	O	O	O
	Success Round	Pre-structuring	O	O	O
	Mindful Moment	Pre-structuring	O	O	O
	Begin Sentence	Signalling	O	O	O
	Meeting Zones	Signalling	O	O	O
	ABSURD	Fun factor	O	O	O
	Baby Writer	Pre-structuring	O	O	O
Infrastructure and artefacts	Gallery Walk	Pre-structuring	O	O	O
	Einstein	Signalling	O	O	O
	Pens	Anticipating mistakes	O	O	O
	Gallery Video	Signalling	O	O	O
	Spatial Design	Pre-structuring	O	O	O
	Visual Documentation	Default value	O	O	O
	Portable Visualisation	Anticipating mistakes	O	O	O
	Visual Echo	Pre-structuring	O	O	O
	PowerPoint Editor	Anticipating mistakes	O	O	O
	PowerPoint Press-B	Anticipating mistakes	O	O	O
	PowerPoint Thumbnails	Pre-structuring	O	O	O
	Stupid Stick	Fun factor	O	O	O
	Fishbowl	Pre-structuring	O	O	O
	Crowd Mobilisation	Signalling	O	O	O
	Open Mic	Pre-structuring	O	O	O
	Throwable Mic	Fun factor	O	O	O
	Bold Label	Signalling	O	O	O
	Spatial Miracle	Signalling	O	O	O
	Nordic Talking	Fun factor	O	O	O

CHAPTER 8

Commitment
Achieving Results through Motivation and Transparency

'What a great feeling', thought the CEO of a start-up company in Zurich when he looked at the Scrumboard in the meeting room, and said, 'It's so good to see what we've accomplished'. At this, his colleague replied with a broad grin, 'We really should have thought of this earlier'. It was only the week before that this start-up had introduced the **Scrumboard** for all projects and meetings. The Scrumboard shows upcoming tasks, tasks underway and completed tasks on a visual template for every project (see Figure 44). In addition, respective team members can be identified using colour coding. The section for completed tasks meant employees could hardly wait to move their Post-it notes from 'underway' to 'done'.

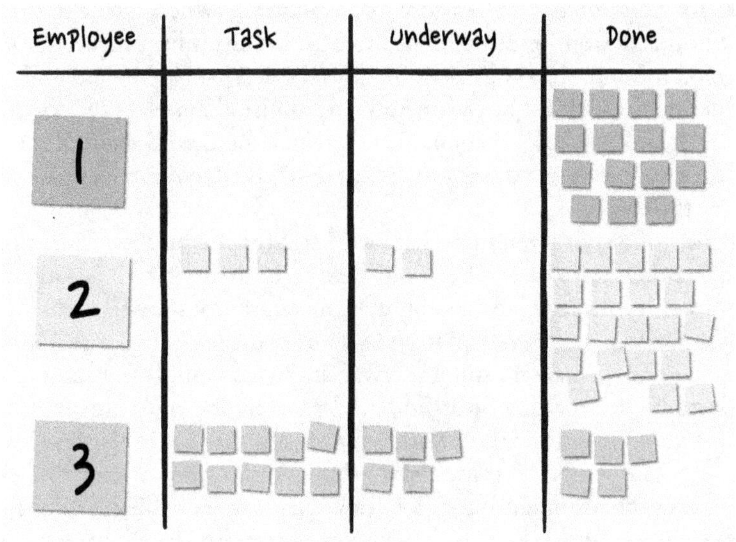

Figure 44 Scrumboard

This triggered some fierce competition in the carrying out of tasks. One team in the software development department even created another column next to the 'done' column with the heading 'done done', into which the tasks could only be moved once their quality had been verified by a colleague (Pries-Heje & Pries-Heje, 2011). One Thursday evening over a beer at the end of the working day, the team came up with the idea of awarding a prize for the most tasks completed and crowning an 'employee of the month'.

The CEO was delighted, having managed to make task completion a matter of personal and professional pride.

Perhaps it was also thanks to what he had read about 'positive meetings' and the importance of mutual support for better health leading to more commitment in the workplace (Heaphy & Dutton, 2008). In the start-up, it had recently become standard practice to use the last ten minutes of a meeting to speed up the completion of assigned tasks through **Peer Coaching**. For this to be productive and for team members to assume the role of a 'critical friend', it is emotionally important for participants to choose their own mentors (Parker, Hall & Kram, 2008). Next, each participant was given five minutes to list the tasks and anticipate any difficulties. Afterwards, everyone sat down in twos or threes so that people could share their challenges and the others suggest possible solutions.

Some teams used the Positive Leadership Game (Dutton & Spreitzer, 2014) for additional problem-solving inspiration, which includes eighty-eight impulses from research on positive leadership. This process not only triggered the completion of tasks but also the active involvement and help of colleagues (who did not want to compromise themselves by not completing their own assignments). So it was not the Scrumboard alone but also the support of other team members that led to the improved completion of the tasks.

'Believe it or not, even then there were still those who didn't manage to complete their tasks', he smiled, 'but we caught them with the spotlight at the start of the meeting'. By spotlight, he meant that at the beginning of the meeting, everyone present had to give a short two-minute progress update – what was done, what was still underway and what would start soon. Since the introduction of this **Spotlight** nudge, even the most uncommitted employees prepared for the meeting and made sure that their tasks were done – because nobody wanted to be shown up in front of everyone else.

'It's exciting', thought the CEO, 'how much we've achieved with three small changes. And not at the expense of others but simply by activating our human resources, so they become more satisfied and productive.'

↑ These three examples illustrate clearly how the subtle use of commitment nudges can lead to a more productive working culture. The Scrumboard is an example par excellence of how transparent feedback can strengthen the personal commitment and self-reflection skills of participants. You can promote these behaviour patterns using nudges where motivation is achieved through *appeals,* such as the Spotlight nudge, or nudges where motivation is encouraged through *fairness* and *transparency,* such as in the Peer Coaching or Scrumboard nudges. When encouraging greater commitment, you can appeal either to common sense or ensure that commitment is fair and transparent – or a combination of both.

The following nudges will show you how you can use both fairness and appeals to persuade participants to be more committed to getting the job done. Now it's up to you to decide for yourself which of these nudges you want to try.

Motivation through Appeal and Reasoning

In addition to the Spotlight nudge, there are other ways to persuade meeting participants to complete tasks through appeal and reasoning. Participants often accept tasks in meetings but then rush off to the next meeting so that by the evening or the following day, the motivation to complete the original task becomes less and less. One way to prevent this is the **Silent Finish** nudge, which allows you to assign the last fifteen minutes of the meeting to participants to work on their assigned tasks and plan their initial steps. This pre-structuring of the Silent Finish nudge works best in combination with the **Closing Round** nudge, where you announce before the silent finish that the closing round will consist of everyone finishing the sentence: 'I will advance this project by doing ... by the end of the week ... '. This gives participants a structure and ensures they have fifteen minutes to prepare for what they will say at the end of the meeting.

If you don't have time for the Silent Finish, you can still use the Closing Round nudge to encourage participants to complete their tasks.

When you need to arrange a series of meetings for one project, then a more extreme version of the Silent Finish – the **Task-Hackathon** nudge – can help participants commit to task completion. Organising a Task-Hackathon is a particularly useful commitment nudge when dealing with large or urgent tasks. The team meets for an afternoon and evening and stays until most of the work has been completed.

People help each other, order in pizza and try not to exceed the 8 pm mark.

If you want to make sure at the end of a Task-Hackathon (or any other meeting) that the remaining tasks are actually implemented, there are two easy ways to this. With the **Signature** nudge, you can note down all agreed-upon decisions and tasks on a flipchart and have everyone present sign it. At Interbrand, this led to senior managers who only attended the occasional meeting honouring their commitment even months later. A similar thing takes place when a restaurant politely asks guests making a reservation to call back if their plans change. In this case, the probability that they will phone to cancel a reservation is much higher than if no request was made. In a study on the willingness of communities to recycle, the simple signing of a pledge card significantly increased recycling behaviour (Burn & Oskamp, 1986). Whether or not you ask participants to sign the flipchart, it is always worth taking a photo of the tasks and integrating it into the follow-up documentation. This **Photo Documentation** nudge uses signals to encourage the rapid completion of tasks. You can take the photo using Microsoft's Office Lens app, then integrate it directly into Word or PowerPoint, making it visible to everyone via the beamer – even during the meeting.

If you want to make sure that employees commit themselves to being productive from the very outset of the meeting, you can use the **Quick Evaluation** nudge.

Before the meeting, place an evaluation sheet on each participant's desk, drawing his or her attention to three points: (1) What contribution could I make to today's meeting? (2) What tasks will I take on? and (3) Was the session useful for me? By asking these questions, you will ensure right from the very start that everyone adapts their behaviour accordingly and pays attention to these points.

In addition to the Quick Evaluation nudge, you can use a highly visible nudge to ensure that all participants commit to taking on and completing tasks they were assigned in meetings. Amazon has an empty chair at every formal meeting, which stands for the customer of the project that is currently being discussed. The empty chair is a signal to all that someone else is relying on the outcome of the meeting. This visual **Empty Chair** nudge is a strong appeal to put yourself in the client's shoes and feel a sense of responsibility for completing the project successfully.

↑ Motivation through appeal and reasoning makes sound sense when you want people to commit themselves in a very hands-on way. In the following section, we will introduce you to some nudges which rely on fairness and transparency to encourage participants to show greater commitment.

Motivation through Fairness and Transparency

If you talk about the meeting agenda according to the Quick Evaluation nudge, it may be worth your while to adopt a practice used by the late Steve Jobs. He would assign a specific person to each item on the agenda, who was responsible for ensuring it was carried out. Steve Jobs set a new standard by calling this person the 'DRI – directly responsible individual'. This **DRI** nudge really must nominate an individual and not a group or department – otherwise, accountability is still unclear. You can determine a DRI for each item when preparing for the meeting so that responsibility is clearly defined. Try to resist the temptation to nominate several people for a task. It really is better to choose just one person to oversee the completion of the task.

An extension of this nudge, which is particularly suitable for complex projects and/or meetings, is the RACI matrix (Jacka & Keller, 2009). This

Figure 45 A nudge in the form of an empty chair to represent the customer
(Source: iStock.com/ER_Creative)

allows you not only to determine the person directly responsible for each task but also to involve other interest groups. With the **RACI Roles** nudge, you can decide on the following roles for each task:

1. The **R**esponsible person, who does the work,
2. The **A**ccountable person, who must ensure that the work is actually done and will be asked to explain themselves if it isn't,
3. the **C**onsulted person, who should be contacted before the work is done or decisions made, and
4. the **I**nformed person, who must be informed after the work is done or after a decision is made.

This will provide more clarity regarding the precise roles of the participants and beyond, and is particularly suitable when there are uncertainties and conflicts regarding tasks and responsibilities.

↓ In Figure 46, you can see the different interest groups at the top, tasks on the left-hand side and the corresponding roles (R, A, C or I) in the matrix.

For complex projects, this allocation of different roles is particularly helpful since it paves the way for efficient cooperation.

Besides the DRI and RACI Role nudges, you can apply additional new standards for your meetings. Avoid a discussion about *whether* participants should complete tasks by setting a new standard of two assignments per

	Executive	Finance	Account Lead	Director	Production	Sales
Business case	R		A		C	I
Finance Plan	A	R		C	I	
Implementation	C			I		A
Launch	I			R		
Event	R	I		A	C	
Video Release			I	A	R	C

Figure 46 RACI matrix to define levels of responsibility

person, which is in line with the principle of distributive justice (Greenberg & Colquitt, 2005). This **New Standard** nudge can be further underlined by handing each participant two Post-it notes at the beginning of the meeting or placing them on each seat beforehand. When someone takes on a task, the Post-its are placed on the flipchart or whiteboard.

With the **Colour Code** nudge, where each employee is assigned a different coloured Post-it, it is immediately clear who is doing what. As an alternative to allocating two tasks, you could also specify that each participant has two (or more) hours available to work on those tasks. An efficient way to ensure that they are aware of the impact and effort and of their functions is the appropriately named **Impact–Effort** nudge.

A Swiss start-up uses this nudge every week, thereby ensuring that the impact and effort of each task are quickly established. This brings dynamism and new ideas to the creation and distribution of responsibilities. For the Impact–Effort matrix (Gray, Brown & Macanufo, 2010), you can draw a 2x2 pattern on a flipchart with the two dimensions, impact and effort, which are low and high respectively (see Figure 47).

First of all, each idea is written individually on a Post-it note. Then the Post-its are placed onto the matrix according to their impact and effort. You could also use the following two strategies to make the analysis more dynamic and develop existing ideas further.

The first strategy aims to boost ideas that have so far had little impact. To do this, look at the ideas in the lower half of the matrix (low impact) and improve on these ideas so that they have a higher impact.

The second strategy is to focus on ideas with low effort and high impact (top left on the matrix) – the 'quick successes'. For this purpose, the team draws another 2x2 matrix inside that section to identify tasks requiring the absolute lowest effort and offering the absolute highest impact. Subsequently, each team member is assigned one of these tasks. Since everyone is involved in task creation, the tried-and-tested categories of impact and effort ensure that these tasks are efficient and – last but not least – the tasks are distributed fairly and everyone is motivated to get involved.

In addition, you can use the **Priority Poker** nudge for a fair and transparent determination of the scope of your tasks. This nudge is particularly useful for complex tasks where the effort required to fulfil them can be interpreted in very different ways (SwissQ, 2017). We'll explain what we mean.

A significant problem facing project leaders is when participants at meetings fail to complete their assigned tasks – or when their efforts are

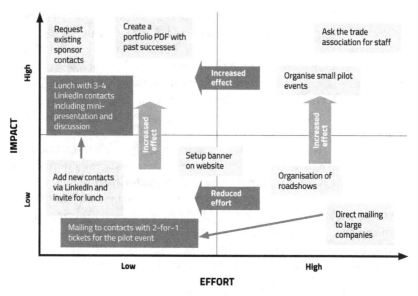

Figure 47 Effort & Impact matrix

substandard. Psychologists call this phenomenon the 'planning fallacy' (Kahneman & Tversky, 1979). This refers to a tendency to underestimate the time needed to complete tasks because of 'optimism bias'.

The physicist Douglas Hofstadter formulated this humorously in Hofstadter's Law: 'It always takes longer than you expect – even when you take into account Hofstadter's Law' (Hofstadter, 2017).

Thanks to the Priority Poker card set, this pitfall can be avoided:

1. To begin with, the person responsible for the task briefly introduces it so that everyone present has an idea of what it is. Each person then receives six cards with different numbers representing the number of hours available to complete tasks.
2. Next, each meeting participant chooses a card with the number of hours he or she considers necessary to complete the task. Then everyone reveals their cards simultaneously.
3. Those with the lowest and highest number of hours must explain their reasons for choosing that number. At this point, different opinions about the scope of the task may already become apparent. For example, if the task is to acquire new suppliers, there may be different expect-ations regarding the number of suppliers in question or in the way they

are contacted. An e-mail quotation request is undoubtedly less time-consuming than a face-to-face meeting. As a result of this initial round, the task can be defined in such a way that, for example, a maximum of five potential suppliers will be asked to submit an offer by e-mail.

4. Using this more accurate task definition, participants now choose a card again and compare results. As a rule, there will be a smaller range of answers in the second round. The person responsible for completing the task accepts either the most frequently estimated number of hours or an average of all the cards shown.

This poker game can be very entertaining as well as helping to define the task and agreeing on a timeframe. The transparency and fairness of this Priority Poker nudge motivate the team to get the job done.

Another way to pre-structure greater commitment to tasks is to use the Eisenhower matrix, which allows you to assign any given task to two categories – 'urgency' and 'importance'. This **Eisenhower** nudge is based on a quote by Dwight D. Eisenhower, 34th President of the United States and a World War II military leader: 'What is important is seldom urgent and what is urgent is seldom important'.

Figure 48 shows you the resulting four-field matrix, in which urgent and important tasks should be *done* immediately, important but non-urgent tasks should be *decided* on, urgent but non-important tasks should be *delegated*, and tasks that are neither urgent nor important should be *deleted*. These categories will help you to achieve greater clarity and better

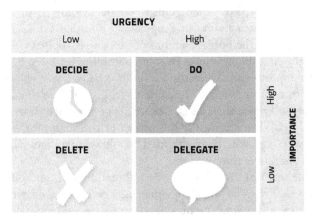

Figure 48 Eisenhower matrix to prioritise tasks effectively

prioritisation of tasks in meetings, leading to a more positive association with the tasks, as well as their completion.

Another positive connotation for completing tasks can be achieved by changing 'deadlines' to 'live-lines'. This increases the degree of embarrassment in the event of non-compliance, which makes you more likely to stick with it and get the job done. Do not set a 'by the next meeting' deadline, but rather a given date, which may also involve others and is *only* about a specific result. A gentler variant of this **Liveline-Not-Deadline** nudge would be to send yourself or others a self-commitment postcard or use an app that reminds you to complete the task before the next meeting.

In addition to this **Personal Commitment** nudge, the **Reminder** nudge is an efficient way for you as chairperson to send a reminder e-mail to all participants three days before the meeting, complete with the open tasks and responsible persons, a (signed) photo of the tasks agreed or with the Scrumboard showing completed tasks. In this way, you can ensure that everyone attending has an overview ahead of the meeting and should still be able to complete their tasks.

↓ If this form of reminder doesn't work, you could try what Phil Jackson – successful basketball coach for the Chicago Bulls and Los Angeles Lakers – did. He had his millionaire players pay small amounts in cash when they were late for training or did not complete their assignments – usually 10 or 20 US dollars. The players grudgingly paid up but found it much more tedious to pay cash directly out of their own wallets on the spot, compared to a larger sum by bank transfer at the end of the season with no effort on their part. Phil Jackson was successful in his case, but it has been shown over time that nudges which encourage good behaviour are more effective than those that punish bad behaviour. In the following sections, you will learn about some digital and non-digital nudges that can be used to visualise the positive actions of meeting participants, rewarding them and enticing them to be even more committed.

↑ By making individual responsibilities transparent, you will encourage your team to commit and, at the same time, give 'visible' space to those who take on and finish their tasks. Acknowledge these people by making it immediately visible – during, at the end or at the beginning of the next meeting – who is pulling their weight. The following nudges will give you visible and audible examples of this.

A notable form of visualisation in combination with audibility comes from none other than Jeff Bezos of Amazon, who introduced a nudge with a high fun factor. To motivate his sales team to generate more deals and to make this visible as well as audible to other salespeople, he installed a **Buzzer** in sales meetings and in the sales office. Whenever someone signed a new contract, he or she was allowed to run to the buzzer and press it enthusiastically.

This was not only great fun for the successful seller, but it also made sure that those who had not yet signed a contract were more motivated to do the same and then go for the buzzer. This nudge – intended for transparency – was so successful that after a while not only sales meetings but the whole day was punctuated by the buzzer. So the red button had to go. But it was not all bad because Jeff Bezos had achieved his original goal of motivating his sales team thanks to the Buzzer nudge.

Besides a physical buzzer in the meeting room, you can also use simple digital nudges to reward positive performance. Send a short compliment or smiley by e-mail, text or WhatsApp when someone has completed a task. Encourage individual positivity through this **Cheer & Applause** nudge and by making the feedback visible. A short personal 'thank you' message is better for motivation than money or other incentives.

↓ Researchers at Duke University conducted a study in which workers at an Israeli semiconductor manufacturing company could choose between a $30 bonus, a pizza voucher or a commendatory text message when they had achieved their goals. On the first day, the pizza voucher proved to be the strongest motivator, but by the end of the week, a congratulatory text message was the preferred reward (Ariely, 2016).

So next time you conduct a task review, remember to praise your colleagues via e-mail, text message or WhatsApp. Even project management tools like Basecamp use digital applause for completed tasks. This Cheer & Applause nudge is technology-based, but it is cheap and gives a lot of satisfaction.

By the way, you don't have to limit your praise to an individual (visibly or otherwise), but motivate entire groups to complete tasks by giving visible feedback. With the **Progress Update** nudge, you establish the practice that any participant can send a message via e-mail, WhatsApp or Slack to the others to share tasks and say which ones have already been completed. This will spur on your colleagues to greater efforts. Through such social norms, you can positively influence your colleagues' performance without having to establish strict rules (Mirsch, Lehrer & Jung, 2017).

As you can see, small digital messages can achieve a lot.

On the subject of digital tools, another ingenious nudge to get meeting participants to complete their assignments is to enter the tasks – including detailed information and finish date – directly into a to-do app such as Todoist. With this **Straight-to-Inbox** nudge, you can clarify 'who has what task and when' at the end of the meeting, while everyone can view this information on their laptop, tablet or smartphone.

Finally, we would like to offer some inspiration for taking the minutes of a business meeting. Some believe that no minutes are needed while others create a single document together, as is the case at Google. We believe that the minutes have added value that goes beyond a chronological summary of the items discussed, so we would like to suggest how you might structure your protocol.

The first option is 'pre-packed' minutes according to the DOCS Box structure, which plays a key role in the meetings toolbox at the European Central Bank.

The DOCS Box structure is about minuting **D**ecisions, **O**pen issues, **C**onfirmations and **S**urprises. In our projects, we have structured meetings with various partners in this way and received feedback to the effect that 'finally we can do something with the minutes and make them interesting to read'. The structure of this **DOCS Box** nudge helps you as the writer of the minutes to condense the various issues into a compact and meaningful structure during the meeting but also allows people who did not attend the meeting to gain a quick overview (for the importance of compact meeting minutes, see Washington et al., 2014).

Discussion topic:
....
....

Date: ....
Participants: ....

Decisions: What was agreed?
....
....

Open issues: What is not yet been agreed?
....
....

Confirmations: Where did we agree and share the same views?
....
....

Surprises: What surprised the participants? What was unexpected?
....
....

Figure 49 The DOCS box as an attractive format for meeting minutes

As a variation and possible addition, it may be worth adding two other sections to the minutes: (1) the number of problems solved and (2) the number of decisions made. We know of a CEO who asks to see these figures from every meeting in his company. As a direct result, participants focus on these two 'KPIs' (key performance indicators) and are willing to solve problems and make decisions. Whether you want to share these figures from the **Number-Solution-Decision** nudge with your own CEO – or whether you are the CEO yourself and think it's a great idea – the matter is now in your hands.

↑ We have demonstrated that you can use nudges to encourage motivation through fairness and transparency in the distribution and completion of tasks, but there are also commitment nudges that motivate through appeal and reasoning if needed. It can be useful to reward a job well done and stimulate greater commitment with a controlled dose of peer pressure (e.g. the Spotlight nudge). Similarly, it can be helpful if you make both responsibilities and completed tasks visible to everyone (e.g. through the Colour Code nudge or Scrumboard).

→ For nudges which prompt commitment, you should always keep fairness in mind, and never forget that commitment nudges are pivotal to carrying forward what has been agreed upon in meetings. One of the biggest challenges you face is ensuring that meetings and commitment are embedded in corporate culture. Dare to be different and create some examples of how to be a committed team member. Show yourself and others what it would be like if it were suddenly fun to carry out tasks or if people no longer discussed the 'ifs' but the 'whats'. Wouldn't that be worth its weight in gold?

→ Be committed and get others on board too. Use these nudges to make commitment the standard and not the exception. Acknowledge not only the tasks still to be completed but those already completed and the people behind them. In this way, you will achieve sustainable commitment. Try out the Spotlight nudge, the Final Round nudge or the DOCS Box nudge – even in a small team of two, commitment can be really motivating.

Commitment Nudges at a Glance

	Nudge	Nudging principle	Yes, from now on	I'll try it out	Maybe later
Appeal and reasoning	Spotlight	Pre-structuring	O	O	O
	Silent Finish	Pre-structuring	O	O	O
	Final Round	Pre-structuring	O	O	O
	Peer Coaching	Anticipating mistakes	O	O	O
	Task-Hackathon	Pre-structuring	O	O	O
	Signature	Signalling	O	O	O
	Photo Documentation	Signalling	O	O	O
	Quick Evaluation	Visible feedback	O	O	O
	Empty Chair	Signalling	O	O	O
Fairness and transparency	Focus Questions	Mistake anticipation	O	O	O
	Results Statistics	Feedback	O	O	O
	Citrus Aroma	Signalling	O	O	O
	Lights Out	Signalling	O	O	O
	Team Check-In	Pre-structuring	O	O	O
	Charge Point	Pre-structuring	O	O	O
	Perspectives Method	Pre-structuring	O	O	O
	Parking Space	Mistake anticipation	O	O	O
	Video Support	Signalling	O	O	O
	Posture	Signalling	O	O	O
	Lights Out	Signalling	O	O	O
	Team Check-In	Pre-structuring	O	O	O
	Charge Point	Pre-structuring	O	O	O
	Perspectives Method	Pre-structuring	O	O	O
	Parking Space	Mistake anticipation	O	O	O
	Video Support	Signalling	O	O	O
	Posture	Signalling	O	O	O

CHAPTER 9

Conclusion and Outlook
Mobilising Meet-Ups

↑ As we there yet? Well, almost. In this chapter, we want to take a brief look back with you and summarise the key findings in such a way that you will be able to apply your new-found knowledge with confidence. We will also take a look at promising developments in the world of meeting management – in terms of both the technology and the psychology of meetings.

← In this book, we have introduced you to the nudging approach as a way to improve the quality of your business meetings. We have assigned a large number of nudges into four different cornerstones, each of which comprises two subareas (see Figure 50). This has made the whole spectrum of nudging principles bear more fruit in meetings. For example, we have frequently used pre-structuring, signalling and feedback nudges to encourage meeting participants to work more productively. At the same time, there are also fun factor, mistake anticipation and new default value nudges for fewer but better sessions, which are well prepared and have a lasting effect.

We have shown that in today's busy world, we need help to stay *focused* – in terms of the number and duration of meetings, as well as the number of participants. But focus also means concentration during meetings in the here and now.

We have seen that even with concentrated work in meetings, *orientation* can be lost (and not just because of disruptive elements) if we do not signal what our primary goal is, where we are in our discussion and how contributions can build on each other. In Chapter 7, we explored a vast range of smart *ways to be involved*, either through infrastructure changes or new procedures and rules. And last but not least, we have addressed the *sense of commitment* and willingness of participants to take on tasks by means of transparency and motivation nudges.

We believe that by applying the principles discussed, you – as chairperson, leader or participant – can facilitate meetings that are worthy of the name Meet-Up.

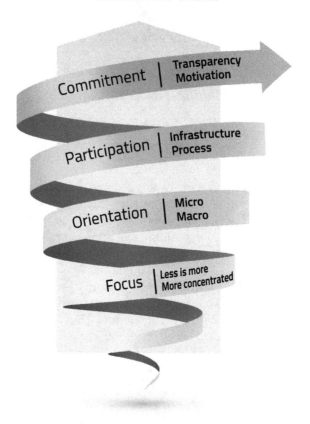

Figure 50 The main elements of the Meet-Up approach in review

↑ Beyond these tricks and techniques, however, we also need a *future-oriented* approach to the issue of meetings, especially with the progressive development of *technological* infrastructure and in terms of understanding what can contribute *psychologically* to successful meetings. We would like to take a brief (and by no means final) look at these two areas in the sense of an outlook.

Meetings and Positive Psychology

At the beginning of the book, we pointed out that meetings are – sadly – often viewed unfavourably. Negative emotions reduce productivity, both

↓ **Box 8 – Strategy Meetings: From Missed Opportunity to Driver for Change**

Speaking of the future, don't forget to allocate sufficient time and space for strategic meetings in addition to your ongoing operational meetings. The last box in this book covers this critical topic.

Another type of meeting that we consider essential is one in which a group of managers reflect together on the strategy of their organisation. In reality, such strategic discussions often miss out on the opportunity to formulate future drives or make adjustments to plans.

Instead of talking about the future, urgent operational problems are discussed and scapegoats sought. Instead of thinking in terms of scenarios and new approaches, a quick consensus and rapid implementation take priority over a measured discussion. However, none of this is conducive to the sustainability of the organisation. How can this be avoided and what do our four cornerstones for Meet-Up success mean for this type of meeting? Here are the most important things to remember about strategy meetings:

Focus: Focus in this context means a radical future-orientation. Under no circumstances should you fall back into purely operational discussions. As part of the team, concentrate on options, scenarios and the strategic consequences of what has been achieved so far. A good nudge for this is to leave the following question permanently visible on the flipchart: 'Will this still be relevant two years from now?'

Orientation: In strategy discussions, especially, it is crucial not to lose sight of the big picture and always to know what discussion you are having and why. Therefore, use the Navicons as a means to signal whether you are still conducting a strategy review (←) or are already thinking ahead (→). Another critical point is the inside-outside orientation. Strategy discussions should discuss not only internal challenges and opportunities but also spend time on external trends and developments. We can also use involvement to help us here.

Involvement: Make sure that strategy sessions also include outside perspectives and that you are not just regurgitating what you already know. For example, include a colleague who has only recently joined your organisation and another who has regular contact with customers. Hang posters with customer quotes, competitor offers or market research statistics in the meeting room to draw subtle attention to the external.

Commitment: Strategy discussions require a transparent exchange of information. You should, therefore, ensure your colleagues provide all relevant information well in advance. Only when the present and past are understood by everyone can the future be usefully discussed. This can be done productively using appropriate infographics or posters, which can be prioritised and discussed at the beginning of the session with the help of Navicons.

'After the strategy meeting is before the strategy meeting.' Make sure that the strategy dialogue continues after the meeting. If possible, you should agree during the meeting on a follow-up date and what needs to happen by then. Two to four strategy meetings per year are now the norm in most organisations.

Whether in a large corporation, a small company or a non-profit organisation, strategy meetings are too important to be left to group dynamics or to chance (see Kwon et al., 2014). Therefore pay special attention to the four areas and prepare appropriate nudges. In this way, a strategy meeting changes from a missed opportunity to a real driver for change.

in preparation and during the meeting itself. We hope that the nudges in this book will help you to have a more positive meeting experience.

In positive psychology, which has advanced rapidly in recent years, you could even go a step further and speak of 'positive meetings', which care for mental and physical well-being and demonstrably achieve a greater commitment from the workforce.

The well-being theory developed by Martin Seligman, the spiritual father of positive psychology, is based on the PERMA principles, which aim to increase well-being in various areas of life. The following summary demonstrates how some of the nudges in this book support these PERMA principles.

P = Positive Emotions

Positive emotions ensure that our view is broadened and we are more open to different perspectives and new solutions. We have already heard from the Dalai Lama that cheerfulness is an important component of any meeting. You can use the **Cheer & Applause** nudge from Chapter 8 to ensure greater appreciation and positivity among your meeting participants. The **ABSURD** nudge from Chapter 7 uses humour and the rewards of helping others to solve problems.

E = Engagement

Engagement refers to the state of high energy that we can experience alone and in groups. We can achieve the highest level of engagement when we are in the flow state, which we already described in the introductory chapter. With the **Think-Pair-Share** nudge, you can ensure raised energy levels by staggering the involvement of individuals and groups. In addition, the **Nordic Talking** nudge can supply lots of energy to small groups by combining physical activity and fresh air with problem-solving.

R = Relationships

We have shown in Chapter 8 that good relationship management in meetings can trigger greater well-being and commitment among participants. With the **Peer Coaching** nudge, you help everyone to support each other in terms of content and, at the same time, strengthen working relationships. You can also use the **Signal Cards** nudge to foster better relationships in meetings. Remember the example of the American engineers in Chapter 6?

M = Meaning

Greater meaning and purpose in life equals greater well-being, and this is especially true when you trigger a positive experience for another person. Think of the **Hollywood** nudge, which allows you to focus on the positive and the potential when giving feedback. Only then can you constructively raise concerns, provided you also offer strategies for dealing with these concerns. Furthermore, the **Meet-Up Checklist** can be used to ensure a meeting is necessary and reasonable for a particular issue.

A = Accomplishments

This is about achieving goals, which is often associated with determination. A good example of this is the **Scrumboard** nudge, which is not only about visualisation but also about making oneself aware of completed tasks and celebrating them. Like the start-up in Chapter 8, you can go as far as crowning an employee of the month for the number of tasks completed. Alternatively, adopt the **Einstein** nudge and use pen and paper to gain new insights and visually record them as an achievement.

↑ When allocating the nudges to the five PERMA principles, it was noticeable that the nudges towards involvement and commitment tend to *promote* positive experiences, while nudges towards focus and orientation tend to *avoid* negative experiences.

As you can see, with the help of nudges, you have the opportunity to create positive meetings that lead to more well-being and greater commitment at work. Mental and physical health is a prerequisite for sustainable productivity and satisfaction at work and in life generally – an issue that is currently gaining importance and will undoubtedly continue to do so in the future.

You can make a valuable contribution by using nudges to make business meetings a positive experience. We wish you and your working environment all the best!

Speaking of our working environment, sooner or later, digital technologies will have a profound influence on our well-being and productivity. It is therefore worth taking a look at some of the major trends in this area.

Technological Developments

New, digital technologies can offer some powerful infrastructure and artefact nudges for your meetings, enabling you to lead your team to greater productivity in meetings. Developments from Microsoft, Ricoh/ IBM and Google show that large interactive screens facilitate lively sessions in which physical and virtual participants can work closely together.

In 2015, Microsoft launched the Surface Hub, an 84-inch monitor designed to simplify virtual collaboration through responsive and natural hands-free input and advanced touch functions. By combining video conferencing, PowerPoint presentations and a whiteboard, this monitor attempts to integrate those who are not physically present at the meeting. The screen causes the chairperson to notice and incorporate contributions from virtual participants just as much as if they were there in the flesh. The permanent visibility of the whiteboard next to the slides encourages participants to note down upcoming additions, questions and comments while keeping an eye on the slides.

In 2016, Ricoh together with IBM and their Watson technology released the 'cognitive whiteboard' – an interactive whiteboard with artificial intelligence. This whiteboard assists participants from other countries with any language barriers through a direct translation of any exchange. Using speech recognition, the system can automatically take notes of conversations or translate different languages into text directly on the screen. The cognitive whiteboard can even guide participants through the agenda and then send them the most important notes from the session.

Google launched its Jamboard in 2017, which they say is only the beginning of a series of hardware products developed for the business world.

According to Google, the Jamboard should be better than a traditional whiteboard thanks to an accurate and fast responding display. The accuracy and authenticity of the drawings on the screen are intended to tempt users to draw directly on the screen, making their thoughts explicit and sharing them (Figure 51).

The visual appearance of the Jamboard is in stark contrast to the grey screens of Microsoft and Ricoh/IBM. The round shapes and way-out colours make the screen look less businesslike and, according to Google, should encourage users to be playful and creative. The rationale behind this is to make creativity and collaboration more fun – a nudging factor not to be underestimated, as we have seen in Chapter 2.

What these three screens all have in common is that they are designed to simplify the sharing of information, combine video and documents, and simultaneously integrate ready-made content, for example, in presentations or ad-hoc visualisations such as sketching on a whiteboard. These features are infrastructure and artefact nudges that are used to promote high productivity in meetings.

Figure 51 With Jamboard, Google wants to tempt users to be playful and creative
(Source: Google)

But it's not just large screens alone that make virtual and physical collaboration more efficient. The Delta Room at PwC in Paris is an excellent example of how the use of large screens with 3D gesture recognition (using Oblong's mezzanine technology) together with a new spatial design can lead to a better meeting experience (Figure 52).

Gesture recognition makes it easier to share content from multiple devices. With a finger swipe on the tablet, content can be immediately viewed on the large screen. Technology like this is a nudge for quick and easy sharing and collating information. At the same time, swift access to information should help participants make faster decisions.

↑ So much for two important trends in the world of meetings – positive psychology and its PERMA approach, and the potential of physical-digital meetings. We have now well and truly come to the end of this book – but allow us one more small transfer nudge in your own interests.

Figure 52 PwC's Delta Room in Paris supports better team decisions (Source: Oblong)

More Courage for Meet-Ups!

If you want to enable other people to bring more focus, orientation, involvement and commitment to meetings, then give this book as a present by using this **Gift** nudge so others can discover and use their favourites too.

Don't forget to experiment with your own nudges and share your experiences with us if you want to. To help you, we have founded a small and friendly online community through our website www .meetup-book.com, which embraces changes to our meeting culture as organisational development.

Now we wish you the same *courage* that Rea Yunen showed at the beginning of the book – the courage to get more out of meetings, to dare for stronger focus, to give more frequent orientation, to facilitate better involvement and to demand greater commitment.

Appendix

Meet-Up ABCs

A for Agenda

'It is not enough simply to have no plan – you must also be unable to follow it.' The exact opposite of this applies to meetings! The agenda of the meeting should not only be clear and permanently visible to everyone, but it should also be adhered to concerning the allocated time. A tool to help you can be found under **T**.

B for Be Focused

During the meeting, make sure that mobile phones are turned off and laptops are closed. Demonstrate appropriate behaviour yourself and use interaction and visualisation to activate all participants.

C for Checklist (for preparation)

What belongs in a meeting checklist? We propose these minimum points:

Need: Does this meeting have the right format?
Participants: Does everyone have a clear role and/or significance for the meeting? Are the relevant decision-makers and specialists going to be there?
Agenda: Is there an agenda? Is it accurate (e.g. is there time for feedback)?
Information: Is the necessary information available?
Time: Has adequate time been allocated to the topic under discussion? Is this appropriate? See point **D** below.

MEET-UP-MANIFESTO

for the 21st Century

Assumptions:

A Meetings take up a large proportion of our working time and are very costly.

B We are dissatisfied with the quality and quantity of our (physical and virtual) meetings and know they could be much better.

Declaration of meeting rights and obligations:

1 We have the right to relevant, productive, focused and constructive meetings.

2 We have the right not to attend meetings to which we cannot contribute, whose topics do not concern us or whose information base is missing.

3 We have the right to short meetings that begin and end on time.

4 We have the right to well-planned meetings and receipt of all the relevant information in advance.

5 We have an obligation to prepare for relevant meetings and implement the decisions taken without delay.

6 We have an obligation to attend meetings on time and to be fully present, active and attentive.

7 We have an obligation to seek solutions constructively and not to misuse meetings as platforms for our complaints or aggression.

8 We have an obligation to consider and implement the latest research findings relating to productive meetings.

That is why we demand:

I No more alibi meetings. Only those who can make a contribution or are directly affected should take part. We will not arrange a new meeting if nothing has happened since the last one.

II No meetings without goals and a permanently visible agenda/time.

III No meetings without the possibility of giving feedback. No meetings without high-quality interaction.

IV Brainwriting (write down, then exchange) instead of brainstorming, and shared visualisation instead of lengthy slide presentations.

V Virtual sessions only with split-screen visualisation, our microphones muted while listening and a comprehension check at the end.

VI No meetings without a brief set of minutes (points discussed & who does what by when).

Figure 53 A wake-up call for a better meeting culture

D for Duration

A productive meeting need not necessarily take one hour. Set a new default value for meetings at 25 minutes and discover that this is quite sufficient for many projects if you concentrate on the essentials. See **F** below.

E for Expectations

It is best to clarify your expectations of the meeting before the meeting begins (e.g. via e-mail) or alternatively as soon as the meeting starts.

F for Focus

Force yourself to have fewer, shorter and smaller meetings, which will lead to greater commitment, better productivity and improved concentration. If these goals are temporarily lost, focusing questions can help too.

G for Ground Rules

The ground rules of a productive meeting are:

1   No meetings without objectives and an agenda.
2   Whenever possible, start and finish on time.
3   At least one record of decisions taken and a 'who does what' list.

H for Hidden Profile

People in meetings tend to tell each other precisely what everyone already knows because it gives them more confirmation. Stasser calls this problem 'hidden profiles'. It can be solved by asking participants to send their exclusive information or views in writing to the chairperson before the meeting.

I for Involvement

How do you involve your colleagues in the success of a meeting? Flipcharts and pens, fruit and coffee, fresh air, good light, a projector and perhaps a pinboard with markers etc. are essential keys to better involvement. But restrictions (e.g. on talking time) or new forms of interaction such as short two-person dialogues also help ensure that everyone can make a relevant contribution.

J for Joker Card

A joker card in meetings can be used to shorten unproductive discussions, to introduce a particularly radical idea or to request a short break.

K for Kind (of meeting)

Trying to achieve too much in one meeting can be counterproductive. It is, therefore, a good idea to signal clearly to all participants what type of meeting this is. Is it about bringing each other up to speed, making decisions, clarifying a problem, the creative generation of ideas or the division of tasks? This is all part of orientation.

L for Leadership

The chairperson need not always be the hierarchically most senior person present.

M for Meeting Spiral

Bad meetings lead to more meetings and are therefore double productivity killers. Avoid this negative meeting spiral by proper preparation and follow-up. Turn the negative spiral of meetings into a positive spiral of improvement through focus (fewer and shorter, but more concentrated meetings), orientation (clear goals, clear discussions), involvement (brief and by all, instead of dominating monologues) and a (transparent) commitment to clear tasks and binding deadlines.

M for Meet-Up

A Meet-Up is a short, intensive (usually voluntary) working meeting where all participants prepare, participate actively and are goal-oriented. Tasks are discussed in an open-minded way and subsequently implemented quickly and responsibly.

N for Nudge

A nudge is a subtle impulse to prompt people towards better (meeting) behaviour. Examples include a large clock on the wall (to encourage time discipline), a flipchart pre-labelled with the agenda or a short feedback note (Was this meeting necessary? Was it well-prepared? Did everyone participate?) We distinguish between different nudging approaches, such as changing default values, pre-structuring decision paths, increasing the fun factor, placing critical information prominently or creating feedback possibilities on what has been achieved.

O for Orientation

Create orientation in the 'meeting jungle' by visualising all your recurring meetings and clarifying which meeting fulfils what primary purpose and how much time (and the number of participants) is really necessary. Also, name the meetings accordingly to make their purpose clear to everyone. Create orientation in each individual meeting using a permanently updated agenda and a clear signal as to what kind of meeting you are currently having (overview, detail, review or planning meeting).

P for Pause

After 20 minutes, our attention often diminishes considerably. Therefore, it can be useful to take a short break every 20 minutes and perhaps discuss hot topics in an informal conversation between two people.

Q for Query Enthusiasts

Unfortunately, these pedants crop up in many meetings. Our advice: take them to one side for a quiet word and explain that – however well-intentioned – this behaviour can be disruptive or unhelpful.

R for Roles

Who is leading the meeting? Who is taking the minutes? Who is sharing direct responsibility and who is only there as an advisor (and for which issues)? Are their roles clear to everyone involved?

S for SPIN

If you can't think of another agenda structure, try SPIN:

1 **S**ituation
2 **P**roblem
3 **I**mplications
4 **N**ext steps

T for Tracker

A visual meeting agenda on a flipchart – also called a tracker – can help maintain focus and keep to time. The agenda must be presented at the beginning and, if possible, a time limit set for each item on the agenda.

U for U-turn

Reverse the logic by starting the meeting (like at Amazon and LinkedIn) with everyone quietly studying the material and making notes on important points. Do not enter the discussion phase until this step has been completed.

V for Vow (Commitment)

Make sure that commitments have been kept by checking at follow-up meetings. Part of this commitment is the preparation of the meeting. The best way to prepare for a meeting is to have a well-formulated text which summarises the situation, the problem and possible options on one page. This can be read by all participants at the beginning of the meeting and then discussed.

W for Which (option to take)

Give people the choice of whether or not to attend a meeting. Several well-known organisations are already doing this with great success.

X for eXaggerate

Some will participants exaggerate how well prepared they are for a meeting – even when they are not. This leads to unproductive discussions. So what can you do? Go back to letter **U**!

Y for Generation Y

During meetings, also pay attention to the specific needs and expectations of Generation Y (those born after 1980). It is especially important for them to get involved and receive appreciative feedback. Let the youngest participants speak first to benefit from their fresh perspective.

Z for Zen (meetings)

Mindfulness, impulse distance, calmness and inner peace are essential prerequisites for successful meetings. Pay attention to your mental state – feelings such as anger or fear – and be cautious but respectful to participants who find it hard to control their emotions.

Signal Cards for Your Meetings

Use the signal cards in this appendix to provide orientation in meetings by allowing participants to use them to visualise their concerns (more or less subtly) without interrupting others. They are part of a more comprehensive set of cards available at www.meetup-book.com.

Parking space: Let's park this issue and come back to it later.

Dead end: This discussion is getting us nowhere, and we should stop now.

Navicon arrow:

Pointing right = Let's discuss what to do next.
Pointing up = Let's discuss the overall context.
Pointing down = Let's go into greater detail.
Pointing left = Let's discuss how this came about.

Joker card: Only constructive criticism of this (maybe crazy) idea is welcome.

Break time: We should take a coffee (or tea!) break ASAP.

Yellow card: That was unfair.

YELLOW CARD

Bibliography and Further Reading

1 Introduction

Mankins, M., Brahm, C., & Caimi, G. (2014). Your Scarcest Resource, https://hbr
.org/2014/05/your-scarcest-resource (Last accessed: 07.09.2020).
Csíkszentmihályi, M. (2010). *Das Flow-Erlebnis: Jenseits von Angst und Langeweile:
Im Tun aufgehen*. Stuttgart: Klett Cotta.
Eppler, M. J., et al. (2016). Zusammen denken: Ein Manifest für bessere
Besprechungen. *OrganisationsEntwicklung*, No. 4.

2 Background

Burmester, H. (2016). Stupser für die innovative Organisation. Wie Nudging die
Organisationsentwicklung bereichern kann. *OrganisationsEntwicklung*, 1, 59–65.
Stasser, G., & Titus, W. (2003). Hidden profiles: A brief history. *Psychological
Inquiry*, 14(3–4), 304–13.
Thaler, R. H., & Sunstein, C. R. (2009). *Nudge: Wie man kluge Entscheidungen
anstößt*. Berlin: Econ.

4 Meet-Up Model

Allen, J. A., et al. (2015). *The Cambridge Handbook of Meeting Science*. Cambridge:
Cambridge University Press.
Shneiderman, B. (1996). The eyes have it: A task by data type taxonomy for
information visualizations. Proceedings of the 1996 IEEE Symposium on Visual
Language, 336–43.

5 Focus

Andrade, J. (2010). What does doodling do? *Applied Cognitive Psychology*, 24(1),
100–6.
Goleman, D. (2015). *Konzentriert Euch!: Eine Anleitung zum modernen Leben*.
Munich: Piper.
Meetings-Imagine. (2017). https://meetingsimagined.com/tips-trends/value-scent-
how-aromatherapy-canchange-your-meeting-better (Last accessed: 20.11.2017).

Mirivel, J. C., & Tracy, K. (2005). Premeeting talk: An organizationally crucial form of talk. *Research on Language and Social Interaction*, 38(1), 1–34.

Spradley, J. P. (2016). *The Ethnographic Interview*. Long Grove, IL: Waveland Press.

Volkema, R. J., & Neiderman, F. (1995). Organizational meetings: Formats and informational requirements. *Small Group Research*, 26, 3–24.

Zoladz, P. R., & Raudenbush, B. (2005). Cognitive enhancement through stimulation of the chemical senses. *North American Journal of Psychology*, 7(1), 125–40.

6 Orientation

Allen, J. A., Beck, T., Scott, C., & Rogelberg, S. G. (2014). Understanding workplace meetings: A qualitative taxonomy of meeting purposes. *Management Research Review*, 37(9), 791–814.

Axelrod, R., & Axelrod, E. (2014). *Let's Stop Meeting Like This: Tools to Save Time and Get More Done*. Oakland: Berrett- Koehler Publishers.

Boden, D. (1995). Agendas and arrangements: Everyday negotiations in meetings. In A. Firth (ed.), *The Discourse of Negotiation: Studies of Language in the workplace*, 83–100. Oxford: Pergamon.

Harkins, P. (1999). *Powerful Conversations: How High Impact Leaders Communicate*. New York: McGraw Hill.

Kauffeld, S., & Güntner, A. V. (2016). Teilnehmer-Typologie. *Organisations Entwicklung*, 4, 29–35.

Schindler, M., & Eppler, M. J. (2002). Vom Debriefing zum kontinuierlichen Erfahrungslernen. *OrganisationsEntwicklung*, 21(1), 58–71.

Schindler, M., & Eppler, M. J. (2003). Harvesting project knowledge: A review of project learning methods and success factors. *International Journal of Project Management*, 21, 219–28.

Weick, K. (1995). *Sensemaking in Organizations*. Thousand Oaks: Sage Publications.

7 Involvement

Azlina, N. N. (2010). CETLs: Supporting collaborative activities among students and teachers through the use of think-pair-share techniques. *International Journal of Computer Science Issues*, 7(5), 18–29.

Colzato, L. S., Szapora, A., Lippelt, D., & Hommel, B. (2017). Prior meditation practice modulates performance and strategy use in convergent- and divergent-thinking problems. *Mindfulness*, 8(1), 10–16.

Dennis, A. R., & Valacich, J. S. (1994). Group, sub-group, and nominal group idea generation: New rules for a new media? *Journal of Management*, 20(4), 723–36.

Doorley, S., & Witthoft, S. (2011). *Make Space: How to Set the Stage for Creative Collaboration*. New Jersey: John Wiley & Sons.

Eppler, M. J., Hoffmann, F., & Pfister, R. A. (2014). *Creability: Gemeinsam kreativ*. Stuttgart: Schäffer-Poeschel Verlag.

Eppler, M. J., & Pfister, R. A. (2010). Drawing conclusions: Supporting decision making through collaborative graphic annotations. Information Visualisation (IV), 14th International Conference, 369–74.

Havas, David A., Glenberg, A. M., Gutowski, K. A., Lucarelli, M. J., & Davidson, R. J. (2010). Cosmetic use of botulinum toxin-A affects processing of emotional language. *Psychological Science*, 21(7), 895–900.

Kangasharju, H. & Nikko, T. (2009).Emotions in organizations: Joint laughter in workplace meetings. *The Journal of Business Communication* (1973), 46(1), 100–19.

Kernbach, S., Bresciani, S., & Eppler, M. J. (2015). Slip-sliding-away: A review of the literature on the constraining qualities of PowerPoint. *Business and Professional Communication Quarterly*, 78(3), 292–313.

Lehmann-Willenbrock, N. K., & Allen, J. A. (2014). How fun are your meetings?: Investigating the relationship between humor patterns in team interactions and team performance. *Journal of Applied Psychology*, 99(6), 1278–87.

Malouff, J. M., Calic, A., McGrory, C. M., Murrell, R. L., & Schutte, N. S. (2012). Evidence for a needs-based model of organizational-meeting leadership. *Current Psychology*, 31(1), 35–48.

Mayer, R. E., & Moreno, R. (1998). A split-attention effect in multimedia learning: Evidence for dual processing systems in working memory. *Journal of Educational Psychology*, 90(2), 312–320.

National Health Service. (2017). www.nhs.uk/news/lifestyle-and-exercise/office-workers-of-englandstand-up-for-your-health/ (Last accessed: 20.11.2017).

Oppezzo, M., & Schwartz, D. L. (2014). Give your ideas some legs: The positive effect of walking on creative thinking. *Journal of Experimental Psychology: Learning, Memory, and Cognition*, 40(4), 1142–1152.

Public Health Ontario, Health Nexus Canada. (2010). *Priority Setting: Four Methods for Getting to What's Important.* Ottawa, ON: Ontario Health Promotion E-Bulletin.

Rietzschel, E. F., Nijstad, B. A., & Stroebe, W. (2010). The selection of creative ideas after individual idea generation: Choosing between creativity and impact. *British Journal of Psychology*, 101(1), 47–68.

Schulz-Hardt, S., & Brodbeck, F. C. (2012). Group Performance and Leadership. WOP Working Paper, No. 2012/4.

Shimojima, A. (1999). Derivative meaning in graphical representations. Proceedings. 1999 IEEE Symposium on Visual Languages, 212–19.

Steiner, V. (2011). *Energiekompetenz.* Munich: Pendo Verlag.

Valentine, E. R., & Sweet, P. L. (1999). Meditation and attention: A comparison of the effects of concentrative and mindfulness meditation on sustained attention. *Mental Health, Religion & Culture*, 2(1), 59–70.

Van Gundy, A. B. (1984). Brain writing for new product ideas: an alternative to brainstorming. *Journal of Consumer Marketing*, 1(2), 67–74.

8 Commitment

Ariely, D. (2016). *Payoff: The Hidden Logic that Shapes Our Motivations.* New York: Simon and Schuster.

Burn, S. M., & Oskamp, S. (1986). Increasing community recycling with persuasive communication and public commitment. *Journal of Applied Social Psychology*, 16(1), 29–41.

Dutton, J., & Spreitzer, G. (2014). *How to Be a Positive Leader.* San Francisco: Berrett Koehler.

Gray, D., Brown, S., & Macanufo, J. (2010). *Gamestorming: A Playbook for Innovators, Rulebreakers, and Changemakers.* Sebastopol: O'Reilly Media.

Greenberg, J., & Colquitt, J. (2005). *Handbook of Organizational Justice.* Mahwah, NJ: Lawrence Erlbaum Associates.

Heaphy, E. D., & Dutton, J. E. (2008). Positive social interactions and the human body at work: Linking organizations and physiology. *Academy of Management Review*, 33(1), 137–62.

Hofstadter, D. (2017). *Gödel, Escher, Bach.* Stuttgart: Klett Cotta.

Jacka, J. M., & Keller, P. J. (2009). *Business Process Mapping: Improving Customer Satisfaction.* New Jersey: John Wiley & Sons.

Kahneman, D., & Tversky, A. (1979). Prospect theory: An analysis of decision under risk. *Econometrica: Journal of the Econometric Society*, 263–91.

Mirsch, T., Lehrer, C., & Jung, R. (2017). Digital nudging: Altering user behavior in digital environments. In J. M. Leimeister & W. Brenner (ed.), *Proceedings of the 13th International Conference on Wirtschaftsinformatik (WI 2017)*, St. Gallen, 634–48.

Parker, P., Hall, D. T., & Kram, K. E. (2008). Peer coaching: A relational process for accelerating career learning. *Academy of Management Learning & Education* 7(4), 487–503.

Pries-Heje, L., & Pries-Heje, J. (2011). Why Scrum works: A case study from an agile distributed project in Denmark and India. In *Agile Conference (AGILE)*, IEEE, 20–8.

SwissQ (2017). Agile Priority Poker, https://swissq.it/en/agile/priority-poker/ (Adapted – last accessed: 20.11.2017).

Washington, M. C., Okoro, E. A., & Cardon, P. W. (2014). Perceptions of civility for mobile phone use in formal and informal meetings. *Business Communication Quarterly*, 77, 52–64.

9 Conclusion and Outlook

Kwon, W., Clarke, I., & Wodak, R. (2014). Micro-level discursive strategies for constructing shared views around strategic issues in team meetings. *Journal of Management Studies*, 51, 265–90.

Seligman, M. (2012). *Flourish – Wie Menschen aufblühen. Die Positive Psychologie des gelingenden Lebens.* Munich: Kösel-Verlag.

Some of our own research on the nudges presented:

Unfinished Presentations Lead to Greater Involvement and Exchange

McGrath, L., Bresciani, S., & Eppler, M. J. (2016). We Walk the Line: provisional icon appearance on virtual whiteboards triggers elaborative dialogue and creativity. *Computers in Human Behavior, 63,* 717–26.

The Sketch Nudge to Make Conflict More Productive

Mengis, J., & Eppler, M. J. (2006). Seeing versus arguing: The moderating role of collaborative visualization in team knowledge integration, *Journal of Universal Knowledge Management,* 1(3), 151–62.

The Restriction Nudge and Its Effect on the Transfer of Experiences

Alexander, E., Bresciani, S., & Eppler, M. J. (2015). Understanding the Impact of Visual Representation Restrictiveness on Experience Sharing: an Experimental Assessment. *Journal of Visual Languages and Computing,* 31, 30–46.

The Navicon Nudge for Orientation in Conversations

Eppler, M. J., Hoffmann, M., & Kernbach, S. (2015). Navicons for Collaboration: Navigating and augmenting discussions through visual annotations. In *Proceedings of IV2015, the 19th International Information Visualization Conference.* Barcelona, Spain.

Templates as Discussion Nudges

Alexander, E., Bresciani, S., & Eppler, M. J. (2015). Knowledge scaffolding visualizations: a guiding framework. *Knowledge Management & E-Learning: An International Journal,* 7(2).

The Sub-optimal Nudges of PowerPoint Presentations

Kernbach, S., Bresciani, S., & Eppler, M. J. (2015). Slip-sliding-away: A Review of the Literature on the Constraining Qualities of PowerPoint. *Business and Professional Communication Quarterly,* 78(3), 292–313.

The Visual Template Nudge to Make Conversations (in Design Thinking Teams) More Productive

Eppler, M. J., & Kernbach, S. (2016). Dynagrams: Enhancing design thinking through dynamic diagrams. *Design Studies,* 47, 91–117.

The Visualisation Nudge to Achieve Greater Attention and Better Recollection of Your Meeting Content

Kernbach, S., Eppler, M. J., & Bresciani, S. (2015). The use of visualization in the communication of business strategies: An experimental evaluation. *International Journal of Business Communication*, 52(2), 164–187.

Index

CPSIA information can be obtained
at www.ICGtesting.com
Printed in the USA
LVHW021404030121
675542LV00009B/211